The Resilience Dynamic®

The simple, proven approach
to high performance and wellbeing

Jenny Campbell

The Resilience Dynamic®
Book Reviews

Jenny Campbell is the expert thought leader on resilience and wellbeing, whose knowledge and application is based on significant academic research and a strong foundation of understanding what is myth and truth about the subject. The Resilience Dynamic® peels back the layers of traditional behaviours in organisations that hold people back from realising their potential and as a result produces mediocre results and relationships. Learn how being resilient can lead to improved self-confidence and increased capacity for change. The gold continues to show through in the many practical, tried and tested exercises and case studies to support personal and, therefore, organisational resilience.

From personal experience of the Resilience Engine, and now the book that both supports and extends the learning, I encourage everyone to put this at the top of their reading list.

Gina Lodge, CEO of The Academy of Executive Coaching

This book is perfect if you are serious about the need for resilience. For anyone prepared to embrace change and to learn how to balance wellbeing and performance, the contents of the book will show you the way. Based on research with case studies and examples, the reader is taken on a journey where the tools and techniques of resilience are made accessible. The stereotypes and myths are challenged and alternative strategies set out – an insightful challenge to all leaders in today's business arena.

Bob Cowie, Chair of Enable

Practical, persuasive, accessible and energising The Resilience Dynamic® *blasts away the accepted myths and helplessness surrounding the concept of resilience and provides realistic tools to help the reader start their journey towards higher performance and more importantly greater wellbeing.*

Carve out some protected time, some 'slow-down space', and allow yourself to think deeply about how your ability to function and succeed depends on your level of resilience at any point in time, and learn how to re-fuel your resilience tank so that you can feel stronger, safer and more able to embrace and even enjoy the changes and challenges in your life!

Jill Vickerman, Chief Executive of BMA Scotland

This is a highly engaging book which successfully teaches the 'art of resilience' in a pragmatic and effective way. Having had the privilege of being coached by Jenny Campbell personally using these techniques, I can unequivocally recommend the tools and the book as a unique and successful approach to achieve greater personal resilience and success.

Jann Gardner, Chief Executive of Golden Jubilee
Foundation Board, Golden Jubilee National Hospital

A very well built journey into the Resilience world. It clarifies with simple examples how resilience clearly drives high performance leadership. The book drove you in deepening your understanding of how resilience can create surplus capacity well beyond coping and bouncing back, towards improving productivity. Jenny teaches you how to measure and interpret resilience as well as develop a practice to find additional deep sources to increase it. A simple to read, rigorous scientific exercise on behavioural modeling based on real business life examples. Powerful.

Matteo Germano, Global Head of Multi-Asset
and Member of Executive Committee, Amundi

This is an important practice and reference book that illustrates 'the resilience way' and demonstrates the real personal benefits accessible to leaders and managers at all stages in their careers. Jenny Campbell analyses the impacts of stress and explains how the negatives can be converted to positives by developing the practices she recommends. Her direct, no nonsense style ensures that ten years' fieldwork and case studies are converted into a comprehensible, no jargon guide which allows the reader to aspire to and practise being 'resourceful, adaptable and energised' on the pathway to 'innovation and excellence in leading change'.

Nick Kuenssberg, OBE FRSE DUniv, Chairman of
Social Investments Scotland, Royal Conservatoire of
Scotland, Frog Systems Ltd, K2L Ltd

Jenny Campbell has written a book that could've made a big difference to me in my startup in the 2000s, if not at the outcome of the project, definitely in changing the personal experience and how I was able to carry on after it had failed. The Resilience Dynamic® allows you to break away from societal preconceptions about resilience and concentrate on actually being resilient. It is a practical guide that I will now recommend to my business school students as they prepare to re-enter their careers with high demands and expectations.

Luis Vivanco, Adjunct Professor of Operations,
IE Business School, Madrid, Spain

This is the century of opportunities and massive shifts, putting us in front of endless options whilst facing multiple and conflicting demands. At this juncture, stepping up our resilience and becoming more adaptive are absolute imperatives. Jenny Campbell in The Resilience Dynamic® *provides an articulated and balanced approach to resilience, shedding light on the 'myths' and the 'realities'. Her methodology allows the reader to appreciate resilience in a wider perspective, develop resilience with a systematic approach, cross that 'resilience gateway' and then learn to apply resilience practices in a dynamic and flexible way. Yes, because in a VUCA world it is essential that we adapt and embrace change – and that is when resilience plays a pivotal role and allows us to adapt and maximise performance in a sustainable way.*

Liana Logiurato, Ernst & Young, Partner, Head of
Chemicals Transaction Advisory EMEIA

Jenny skillfully points us to the connection between resilience and cultivating a mind that is present, curious and kind. It's neurophysiological. At its best resilience training of this kind increases our ability to access flow and sustainable peak performance and cultivates our capacity for adaptation, growth and flourishing in a world that is constantly changing.

Mark McMordie, Author of *Mindfulness for Coaches* and CEO of The Conscious Leader

This book explains why resilience is important for us all, whatever we are doing. I found it an easy read: interesting and useful. It made me think about my own and others' resilience, how it changed with time and in different situations. Understanding our level of resilience enables an assessment of the chances of successfully delivering change. The Resilience Dynamic® *helps us to understand both how to develop reliance and to recognise the barriers to it – invaluable when preparing for change, whether that be a major business change or a personal one.*

Janet Unsworth, Chair of Four Square,
NED of Student Awards Agency Scotland

First published in Great Britain by Practical Inspiration Publishing, 2019

ISBN   978-1-78860-108-5 (print)
         978-1-78860-107-8 (epub)
         978-1-78860-106-1 (mobi)

Practical Inspiration
PUBLISHING

Contents

Foreword

We are living in a world of profound change, challenge and
uncertainty in all aspects of life. We experience all too often
unforeseen disruption amid the social, political, economic,
technological and environmental systems that govern our lives.
Disruptions occur in a quickening and often erratic manner,
which makes them difficult to predict. The demand for swift
adaptability is felt in every domain. Thus, there is the demand
for resilience.

This has severe implications for leaders and managers in
their personal and professional lives. Organisations, leaders and
politicians have enormous power to lead breakthrough change in
the world and thus help address the myriad of challenges that we
face. This requires deep personal resilient leadership.

Resilience has been defined many times over by different
schools of research, but at its heart it is the capacity of a system,
enterprise or person to maintain its core purpose and integrity
in the face of change. Change is difficult, and the statistics
abound with failed change initiatives. People do not naturally
resist change. They resist the pain of change and the fear of the
unknown. This is important to remember in order to find the
benefit and opportunity in the change. Change cannot happen
without a sense of trust and security, and so it is essential for
leaders to create an environment where psychological safety
flourishes.

My own work shows how Secure Base Leadership is
fundamental in creating this psychological safety. Secure base
leaders enable their followers to transform their anxiety and

fear into courage towards something meaningful. They unleash astonishing potential by building the trust, delivering the change, and inspiring the focus that underpins high performance.

The concept of secure base leadership aligns fully with the fundamental basis of resilience as Jenny Campbell so brilliantly describes in *The Resilience Dynamic®* as the source of your 'resilience river'. Other skills of resilience converge around psychological safety in order to deliver sustainable high performance in times of change and high anxiety.

There is so much hope that resilience can be fostered. Our brain's natural impulse to survive can trigger deep levels of thriving. Many of the early theories of resilience stressed the role of genetics. Some people are just born resilient, so the arguments went. An increasing body of empirical evidence, including that of The Resilience Engine, now suggests that personal resilience is more widespread, learnable and teachable than previously thought. Our resilience is rooted in our beliefs, our character, our experience and our values. Most critically it is fostered in our habits in relation to both mindset and behaviour.

I have known Jenny since her MBA days at IMD business school in 1997 and since then in her stewardship of the IMD Alumni in Scotland. Her rigorous research on resilience, plus her team's sound experience, help destroy many myths about resilience. *The Resilience Dynamic®* dissolves the complexity of the subject, making it transparent, accessible and provides an approach that leaders and managers can easily apply. Jenny presents a truth that we all need to hear.

Jenny has given me fresh insight into how leaders can face situations demanding resilience when small or great challenges occur. It is rare after so many years in the field of high-performance leadership for me to discover something genuinely new and insightful – *The Resilience Dynamic®* is exactly that.

With this book resilience becomes learnable, straightforward and a tool to address any challenge. It is a must-read for all leaders wanting to maintain their own high performance and that of the teams they are leading.

George Kohlrieser

Professor George Kohlrieser is a clinical psychologist and hostage negotiator and is Distinguished Professor of Leadership and Organizational Behavior at the International Institute for Management Development, in Lausanne, Switzerland. He is creator and director of the High Performance Leadership Program (HPL) and the Advanced High Performance Leadership Program (AHPL). He is a media commentator and author of the internationally bestselling books *Hostage at the Table: How Leaders Can Overcome Conflict, Influence Others, and Raise Performance* and *Care to Dare: Unleashing Astonishing Potential through Secure Base Leadership*.

He is a consultant to global companies and institutes and has worked in over 100 countries spanning five continents.

Introduction

'How to keep resilience high? Respect it.'

Please note that all quotes throughout the book unless specifically stated are taken from Resilience Engine resilience research interviews, 2007–2009, 2011, 2013, 2015, 2017.

Who Is This Book For?

What has made you pick up this book?

Perhaps you are a leader or manager of others and wondering what you can do to enable higher performance in your team without draining their wellbeing. You see resilience as the way.

In some organisations resilience has gained a bad name: staff consider that resilience means toughing it out, and anything badged as resilience is just another way of saying you have to do more work with less. That view of resilience, of steeling yourself to something or toughing it out, negates wellbeing in the process. It is wholly inappropriate. Just to be clear, being tough is not being resilient. Real resilience encompasses wellbeing and high performance. This book will show you what that means.

The book offers a theory of resilience based on ten years of research. It includes the top insights into the barriers and enablers for resilience, with tools to put these into practice. You will find the theory both simple and profound; it cuts through a lot of the noise and misconceptions of resilience. Stories are woven throughout the book which illustrate what resilience is and isn't.

Note that Part 1 of the book is wholly dedicated to Busting the Myths of Resilience. These chapters in themselves may help you understand how you might enable resilience in others.

Perhaps you are considering your own wellbeing in the midst of trying to feel successful.

The Resilience Dynamic® is for you if you are up for learning how to become more successful whilst maintaining great health. You have to be curious and you need to be able to give yourself some thinking space for the ideas in the book.

The book will serve you well if you're prepared to open up to the truth of the ups and downs of resilience, and have a genuine appetite for applying the research insights. The benefits of the book are only realisable if you become more confident in them; that means trying them out for real. This is part of the Resilient Way.

The bottom line? You can embrace higher performance and enjoy feeling healthy. You can experience what Daniel Goleman and Mihaly Csikszentmihaly call flow.[1,2] Within The Resilience Engine we talk about the client's 'resilience gateway'. We work with clients on one side where everything seems complicated. On the other side, it's much simpler: you create a set of resilience habits, what we like to call a resilience practice, and from this basis, things fall into perspective. With a resilience practice you have more energy, feel healthier, and connect with more things that matter to you (and let go of the rest). Altogether, it's simple on the other side. But you do have to cross the gateway, and that first step takes energy and commitment.

A word of caution about the book and whether it may or may not be for you. If you're looking for a quick fix, this isn't the book for you. There is no one silver bullet to resilience. If you're looking for just the theory without wanting to put much into practice, this book is not for you. Whilst a strong, evidenced resilience theory is given here, it comes to life for each individual in very personalised ways. That means as a manager or leader, you need to consider how to enable your team to manage their own resilience. It's about them taking responsibility, and you enabling that. The same goes for you. Your first step to a higher resilience is you taking responsibility for you.

Please note that the whole book is written to enable you to do this. Contrary to the norm within academic literature, where the third person is deployed, the second person, 'you', is used throughout. The Resilience Engine's experience is that many people talk **about** resilience as a way of avoiding connecting directly with their own resilience. We have found that addressing 'you' directly interrupts this 'cognitive bypass'.

Your Start Point

Would you describe yourself as resilient? Think about it. Maybe? It depends? The Resilience Engine has been researching resilience for over ten years and works with thousands of people in all walks of life. Here's a sample of how our clients reply to the question:

o *I am not sleeping so well, I'm not really sure if I could claim to be resilient when my head is spinning with everything in the middle of the night!*
o *I cope really well with stuff.*
o *I used to feel I was, but I feel so overwhelmed by everything in work, I just don't get a minute.*
o *Everyone just is busy-busy-busy round here, it's a badge of honour now, everyone says it. Stress is just accepted as the norm.*

○ *Quite resilient. I get through setbacks. Well, obviously depending on what it is, but yeah pretty much, I can punch through.*

○ *To be honest, I don't feel resilient at all right now. My partner is encouraging me to get help, but I haven't done anything yet.*

Here's a different kind of language:

○ *I feel really well, yes, really satisfied with where I'm at.*

○ *I am so much better, I have my mojo back! That is the basis!*

○ *Well, I know I'm resilient now, I have enough capacity for everything I want to do, and yes, there are tough challenges, but Friday nights I can sit with my friends and leave all the work. It wasn't always like that but it feels much easier now than when I was doing battle.*

○ *I definitely invest in it all the time. I do yoga; I run; when I'm tired I rest. And somehow all that means I am able to do my job and my studies, all with the family. It's quite amazing, I feel good!*

○ *When it goes down, I make adjustments immediately, I can spot it.*

So many different responses! What is resilience exactly then?

The Definition of Resilience

The definition of resilience is thoroughly explained in Chapter 5 of the book. In short:

Resilience is your ability to adapt.
It's your capacity for change.

Resilience does include Coping and Bounceback. It needs perspective and humour, self-acceptance and support. But it's not any of these things independently; resilience integrates all of these factors and more. It's both simpler and more strategic as a result.

When your resilience is lower, you don't have as much capacity for change. When it's higher, you can generate different options, you can adapt your solution in the moment as you see it working or not, you can learn, and you have capacity left over for other stuff. It feels entirely manageable. Indeed those with the highest level of resilience feel at ease, no matter what is going on.

Leaders need to develop leadership skills. However, once you have the necessary skills and experience, you need something else, the capacity to get hold of these skills whenever you want and need them. This takes adapting to circumstances every day. Leading for resilience means embedding resilience thinking in your leadership habits. This is the Resilient Way.

The outcomes of resilience are both wellbeing and high performance, or success, in whatever domain. Investment in resilience is investment in wellbeing; resilience acts like a buffer to the negative side of stress. High resilience means more energy, perspective, capacity and clearer focus on what is energising and motivating.

Part of resilience building relies on deeper facets such as beliefs and attitudes; these will need some of your attention. To start off with, however, there are very practical enablers that will immediately boost your resilience. The good thing is that resilience is learnable by everyone. This book is all about that, placing our ten years of learning into your hands.

Why Focus on Resilience Now?

82% SAY THAT **RESILIENCE** DEMANDS ARE **HIGH** AND **10%** SAY IT'S MANAGEABLE*

*Stats are from AoEC poll online.

During 2018, in partnership with the Academy of Executive Coaching,[3] The Resilience Engine carried out a survey on the demand for resilience in the workplace. With over 200 respondents we think the results were a shock.

A whopping 82% say that the demand for resilience is high.

44% of people say the demand is high and rising.

Only 10% say it's manageable.

The survey results are the first hard proof of a trend that resilience levels are severely under threat. The experience of The Resilience Engine showed until recently that the majority of the working population experience resilience levels that are 'ok' – sometimes Coping, sometimes higher, but definitely at a level where things were manageable. The data from this 2018 survey is the first hard evidence of a trend we have been experiencing in our practice in the last three years: that resilience levels of the working population are slipping.

You will see more statistics throughout the book that back up and explain in more detail what is behind this slide backwards. Look at Chapter 7 in particular, on stress, and the percentage of people who cope and who don't cope.

The overall results make the case for investing in resilience a no-brainer.

The Structure of the Book

The book is split into three parts:

Part 1 Busting the Myths of Resilience

Part 1 of the book unpicks the cultural myths that exist around resilience. Reading this may unlock your curiosity, or may alter your own assumptions of the 'right' way to be.

Note that if you are indeed hooked or believe any of the Myths of Resilience, you will inhibit your resilience and your resilience potential. Each one is worth checking out, even if it's just to say it's not one of yours!

The Myths of Resilience chapters may challenge your thinking deeply, and you may initially reject some of the discomfort that this brings. Notice if you do. What are you hanging onto? By hanging onto this, what do you gain?

Each chapter of Part 1 is written with a common structure as follows:

Chapter Overview
The Resilience Scene
The Problem
The Resilient Way
Applying the Resilient Way
Stories of Resilience (where applicable)
The Bottom Line

Please note throughout the book that all exercises are copyright of The Resilience Engine 2019. If you would like to know more about how we can help you apply resilience in your organisation, please see the Resources section.

There are the four Myths of Resilience that are busted:

Chapter 1   Myth 1: Resilience Is Being Tough
Being tough ends up creating the conditions for rigidity. This is the opposite of adaptability, your real resilience.

Chapter 2   Myth 2: Resilience Is Having More Control
An oft-quoted condition of resilience by both writers and psychologists is control. However, being adaptable enough to let go of the need for control is the truer pathway to resilience.

Chapter 3   Myth 3: You Need Confidence for Resilience
Again it is often quoted in many self-evaluations and other mechanisms around resilience that you need confidence to have resilience. There are different facets of confidence, and the relationship with confidence is in fact two-way.

Chapter 4   Myth 4: Driving Efficiency Delivers the Highest Productivity
A more complex myth to describe, but understood experientially. When you are chasing down productivity by trying to improve the efficiency of your processes and your people, it will work only up to a point. Thereafter driving efficiency is no

longer possible. Resilience underpins that next level of productivity needed.

Enjoy myth popping!

Part 2 The Resilience Engine Research Insights

Part 2 of the book explains the core research insights from the ten years of The Resilience Engine's work in the field. You will discover one of the core research models, The Resilience Dynamic®, which explains what resilience is and its nature and implications, including gender differences. You get the chance to consider your own resilience using this model as a lens. Then there are deep dives into the implications for stress and change, and how resilience does indeed mean your capacity for change.

Chapter 5   The Resilience Dynamic®
This is the first and most used research model from The Resilience Engine which explains what resilience is and the strategic implications of different resilience levels.

Chapter 6   The Different Levels of Resilience: Where Are You?
This chapter starts with an easy self-evaluation then delves into each resilience level in detail including the relationship to stress, change and control.

Chapter 7   More Resilience = Less Stress
Stress is often the reason why people start to invest in resilience. But what is stress, and how does resilience relate to it?

Chapter 8   Change and the Resilience Gap
               This chapter shows through both the theory and
               more extensive stories how resilience really *is* the
               capacity for change.

Each chapter of Part 2 is written with common sections including:
     Chapter Overview
     The Resilience Scene
     The Bottom Line

Thereafter section headings differ according to the research insight being explored. The Resilient Way is weaved throughout each chapter.

Part 3 How to Support and Develop Your Resilience

Part 3 of the book is about how to apply what you have discovered so far for yourself and for others. You will explore the Top Enablers of resilience. Detail is given about what to do at each resilience level.

If you are also considering others in your team and how to support their resilience as you go through this book, remember to look at the resilience levels pertinent to them.

Chapter 9   Top Enablers of Resilience
               This chapter examines the Top Enablers of
               resilience in detail. These are being present;
               energy; learning; and purpose. The theory and
               some examples of how to apply the theory are
               given.

Chapter 10   What to Do for Each Resilience Level
This is a summary chapter that you can go straight to after your self-evaluation in Chapter 6. Each main resilience level is considered, and insights and tips are given for all the top resilience enablers.

Each chapter of Part 3 is written with common sections including:
Chapter Overview
The Bottom Line

Each chapter is structured thereafter according to the tools and ideas being explored. Part 3 of the book is all about how to apply the Resilient Way, so you will find it everywhere in these chapters!

End Words: Resilience as a Practice

Finally, there is a summary of the key insights of the book, and a way of integrating these in their totality into a resilience practice. It's about how to stop getting caught in a one-hit wonder that will serve you and your resilience only in the short term. If you want both high performance and wellbeing, these last words will help you embed the ideas of this book into a resilience practice that you can make your own.

Tips for Approaching Your Own Resilience

Be aware that most leaders and managers will take out what they need for themselves at that moment and think they've got the whole thing, that they've cracked resilience! Any conclusions and actions you take today will of course stand you in good stead. However, there are a few caveats for your learning today.

o If you are reading this in a position of leadership in any domain, discovering the implications for all the resilience levels will help you enable others more effectively.

o Now and in the future, your own resilience will go up and down. So whatever your own evaluation of your resilience (via Chapter 6 and the Resilience Check-in© from www.resilienceengine.com), I recommend that you glance through the information about other resilience levels so you are equipped for what to do when you experience them.

o For maintaining your resilience in the long run, you need to build resilience habits into your daily rhythm. Your practice of resilience needs to be sustainable, not some kind of theoretical set of New Year resolutions that dwindle to a small plop sometime mid-February or March.

o Extending your resilience is based on ongoing learning: you need to keep learning new stuff and unlearning old stuff. At some point, your resilience will be 'context free' – you'll have learnt what you need to including how to learn well, and so you will just be resilient.

o **Then most important of all.** Today, now, whilst you are reading this book, your resilience is at a particular level. And that level may mean you have capacity for learning only a certain amount. You won't get the whole lot in the first sitting.

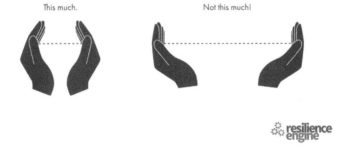

This much.   Not this much!

So why not accept that limitation? Enjoy reading 'lightly'; don't 'try' or overextend your efforts in any way. Follow your nose, enjoy the experience, see what you feel most energised by. Know that you are going to come back to the book again another day.

My wish in the end for you is to really connect with your resilience in an easy way. You will feel better, more confident, and succeed more in what is important to you. That means you will feel more at ease, no matter what's going on.

May your resilience be with you!

Part 1

Busting the Myths of Resilience

Chapter 1

Myth 1: Resilience Is Being Tough

'I don't like self-absorption.'

'There are no mistakes, only opportunities.
Resilient people always reframe mistakes.'

Chapter Overview

This chapter sets out to bust one of the greatest myths of resilience: that it's about being tough. Whilst being strong is an outcome of resilience, being tough is not. Toughness leads to brittleness, the opposite of adaptability.

The chapter will help you connect with your own perceptions of resilience and toughness. It sets out how you can so easily get caught between unhelpful polarities of good versus bad in relationship to many drivers behind resilience, like being right versus wrong, or strong versus weak. It offers the Resilient Way, an alternative view to this polarisation that embraces a more flexible approach.

Finally, you then get the chance to review this kind of new thinking for yourself via reflective exercises.

The Resilience Scene

Hands up, do any of the following statements resonate with you? Or are they part of your organisation's culture?

Don't show your emotion unless you're happy and smiling.

Just say everything is 'fine'.
Don't show you are feeling vulnerable.
Don't show you are stressed.
Don't show you don't know.
Beat yourself up for being so stupid, but only after they have gone.

Do show when you've punched through the challenge.
Do show when you've beaten the opposition.
Do show when you're ok.
Do show when you're feeling smart.
Do show when you've done a lot of smart things.

Any of these statements running around your own head? Unvoiced possibly, but still driving your action? Do any of these drive your organisation? You may have a lot of learnt values from your upbringing, your workplace, your friends. You may collectively live this kind of culture. And these result in a set of values, not necessarily your own, that drive the way you live.

It ends up a bit like a set of polarities that you have to choose sides on:

Good	vs	Bad
Strong	vs	Weak
Win	vs	Lose
Right	vs	Wrong
Control	vs	Out of control
Keep going	vs	Give up
Power	vs	Powerless
Knowledge	vs	Don't know (aka stupid)
Hard	vs	Soft
Unemotional	vs	Emotional
Just do it	vs	Try

What about you?

 Write down

Go through the attributes on the left-hand side, the Good side, and tick which you are drawn towards.

 Review

How many out of the Good ten are you strongly pulled towards? What thoughts do you have whilst doing this exercise?

The Problem

The mantra becomes 'If you want the Good side, you need to embrace all of the Good behaviours'. What an effort involved! No failure accepted, have to keep going at all costs, got to know-know-know, got to be ok in front of everyone.

The alternative? Not the Bad side, please! Many of the attributes on the right hand side are unattractive depending on your life values and those around you. In fact your primary motivators may be about being driven away from these – you'd do anything to ensure you don't appear weak, wrong, a loser.

 Write down

Go through the attributes on the right hand side, the Bad side, and cross through those you dislike.

 Review

How many of the ten attributes on the Bad side do you find distasteful?
How many do you really abhor?
What thoughts do you have whilst doing this exercise?

Becoming aware of whether you are drawn towards or driven away from[4] in these matters is part of the deeper matter of resilience building. Being driven away is a temporary state: when you are close to the thing you want not to be, you create action to shift away. Once you are further away, you ease up the action a little; indeed you may stop it altogether.

Take the example of not wanting to be overweight. Weight management measures kick in strongly when the person is feeling overweight, what they might refer to in their internal self-talk as 'fat'. They dislike feeling like this so move away from it, but their efforts to lose weight decrease and indeed stop altogether once the danger of feeling 'fat' is gone:

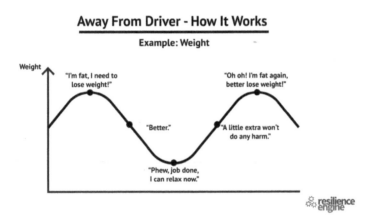

Away From Driver - How It Works

Example: Weight

Weight

"I'm fat, I need to lose weight!"

"Oh oh! I'm fat again, better lose weight!"

"Better."

"A little extra won't do any harm."

"Phew, job done, I can relax now."

resilience engine

The you-have-to-be-tough mantra may come from either side, Good or Bad, but in The Resilience Engine's experience, this myth is fuelled most strongly where someone has an 'away driver',[4] to ensure they don't look weak or stupid. This 'away from' engenders a kind of superhuman, always-on effort to ensure you appear the opposite of what you consider Bad:

If you feel you don't know enough	→	you aim to know lots and lots!
If you feel like you're emotional	→	you aim to hide your emotions.
If you feel you just can't go on, and think this is weak	→	you do the opposite, you go straight back with force, without necessarily changing anything. It's as if you're using your own self as a battering ram. And what gets battered is your resilience including your wellbeing.

The 'hijack'[5]

A lot of energy is spent making sure you don't fall into looking like anything on the 'Bad' side. The level of hold that this can have on you is intense. As George Kohlrieser describes in 'Hostage at the Table',[5] you can get 'hijacked'. Our partners, The Healthy Workforce, talk about the 'amygdala hijack'. This is when you suffer from brain freeze because of sensory overload and being emotionally charged. It's where the cortisol, the 'stress hormone', shoots up whilst the oxytocin, the 'cuddle hormone', your feel-good hormone, shoots down. See Chapter 7 for more. The Resilience Engine observes this kind of 'lock' in many situations: in work, in home life, in decision making, in the dealing with difficult stuff, in planning a new process.

Culturally, whether in your workplace or in your communities, this can be massively exaggerated when looking at groups and teams.

This is how it is amongst team members who have learnt that failure is not acceptable. They work always to ensure success and that in turn might mean subtly toning down expectation or setting goals that are, whilst comfortable, not that motivating. Thus mediocrity gets borne.

Or the team that can't handle emotion. Emotion or being emotional is bad. So don't show it, keep it in, even if it eats you. Cramming your emotions down and down inside into some inner deep pocket with a strong zip so that it stays shut is simply unhealthy: not only do you not honour what you need in the moment, you risk three other much longer-term health and performance-impacting issues:

○ The first is personal but has a big impact on others – emotions that are tucked away bubble up or even boil up at unexpected times, and in situations that don't merit their full force.

 Thus you can be really angry when one of your team casually challenges a decision you make, and instead of pushing back on their challenge in an appropriately casual manner, you ROAR at them. It's not because of that particular challenge, but because of the inner strength of resentment about other criticism levied at your door that hasn't been dealt with and has been eating away inside.

○ The second, for the whole team, is that you miss the possibility of high performance. A high performing team will recognise, honour and develop the emotional side of the team's relationships, to be in service of one another and their overall goals. Not honouring emotions means opportunities for high performance get missed:
 • Emotional safety through trust is denied. Emotional safety is needed to say 'I don't know'.

- Debate and challenge is denied. This naturally aims to shift the status quo (and therefore destabilises what has been safe thus far) of the team.
- New ideas and perspectives are not generated. Innovation is curtailed.

Note that embracing emotion within a team doesn't mean sitting around crying or spending ages in deep, emotional sharing. Honouring emotions can be done briefly – a short explanation, a question or supportive statement, a moving to recognise the impact, and an accommodation and potentially specific support.

o The third and last major effect of denying emotions is again personal: you prevent yourself from developing the awareness required for you to understand the emotion, and what you need from it. For example, you may feel angry but just need a hug. Or you may feel angry and recognise that the level of anger is greater than the situation merits, and it's really that you're exhausted and everything is out of perspective. So instead of addressing the anger, you need to address your tiredness.

Being resilient means spotting what you actually need, rather than where your reactions take you. When someone else upsets you, instead of seeking justice or getting angry, you let go of the anger. If you are mad with yourself, it means letting yourself off the hook. Being resilient often means accepting that it's time to rest. That takes self-awareness.

Developing self-awareness towards self-acceptance is one of the inner biggies of resilience.

The Resilient Way

Holding on intensely to a singular option, either away from 'Bad', or towards 'Good' behaviours, is a brittle approach. It is the opposite of adaptability, a resilient way of being. The Resilient Way is altogether different:

Good	Bad		Resilient Way	Unresilient Way
Strong	Weak		Self-acceptance and with voice where safe Plus the grace to wisely use the power that comes from self-acceptance	Without voice
Win	Lose		Learn	Bypass the learning Stuck in learning short-cuts that stop change being effective
Right	Wrong		There are many 'right' solutions Enquire	One way only, often my way is the only way Have to be seen to know
Control	Out of control		Take responsibility and accountability for what you can, let go of the rest	Shirking responsibility and accountability Placing blame on others

Keep going	Give up		Expect to change path to achieve same goal Change will be driven by data gathered along the way The resources needed for the change identified and made available	Keep going no matter what (on the same solution) OR Give up without knowing why and what
Power	Powerless		With power that comes from confidence, synergistic with resilience Plus the grace to effect that power wisely	Without power Without voice
Knowledge	Don't know		I can learn	I must know Not knowing will make me seem stupid
Hard	Soft		Flexible	Inflexible
Unemotional	Emotional		Accept and honour all emotions whilst remaining resourceful	Hiding or blocking emotions
Just do it	Try		Experiment and learn with openness and curiosity	Try, try, try

11

Applying the Resilient Way

Which is more attractive?

© The Resilience Engine 2019

You can do this as a solo or team exercise.

Step 1

✐ **Write down**

Circle the items in the Resilient Way column that you are attracted to.

🔍 **Review**

For the Resilient Way, how many out of the ten are you strongly pulled towards?

Step 2

✐ **Write down**

Circle the items in the Unresilient Way column that you find least attractive.

🔍 **Review**

For the Unresilient Way, how many do you really abhor?

Step 3

⇦ **Change**

Which list do you want to operate from: the Good/Bad or the Resilient Way/Unresilient Way?

The key difference in living the Resilient Way is being intentional. What new intentions might you consider in contexts where you are stuck between the Good versus Bad?

✓ **Commit**

What intention for yourself and your resilience will you now hold?

Stories of Resilience

John

John is a senior leader in a large leading corporation which operates in a very competitive marketplace. John has got to his position on what he knows, and his ability to translate that directly and quickly into action within the organisation. John is very bright and runs a good ship. He is aware of the speed of his processing and that his style is quite dominating, and has managed across the years to find a comfortable middle way, where he consults with others before making decisions. Everything in the end still goes through him, but he is happy that he has improved his delegation skills.

John has new team members who are very different to him. They are also bright and knowledgeable, and are a lot more comfortable in relying on the opinion of their staff without having to know the detail. John doesn't like this, and finds it quite easy to catch them off guard. John is showing that his resilience, whilst high, is not as high as he imagines it to be. He might be caught at the level that The Resilience Engine calls Bounceback.[6] (See Chapter 5 for a full definition of Bounceback.)

His behaviour is beginning to grate on his team, and he suspects the recent resignations of two of his senior people are related, although the reasons quoted were quite different. John doesn't really see that he can change much after all these years, and just decides to get on with it. He has a nasty surprise, however, when his new executive director gives him a difficult performance review and tells him he needs to change his management style otherwise the company will end up losing more good people. John is at a loss as to what all this means and what he can do about it. John feels stuck, and is very angry with the whole situation.

John's ability to adapt is low, and he resents being forced into a situation where he doesn't know what to do. His resilience is related to his ability to control things, and when he can't control, his resilience plummets. Instead he gets caught in anger and resentment, and with this there is an increased danger of his performance dropping. John's resilience falls back, sometimes at Bounceback when he is in his comfort zone, but overall lower, where he is having to cope with this new situation and the pressure on him to change.

Without learning how to adapt, John's performance will be stuck and he risks his position in the company. It's make or break time for him.

⌣ The Resilience Lens

How much did John's story resonate with you?

John is clearly a high performer and proud of that. Which blind spots does he suffer from that constrain his resilience?

What might your blind spots be that hold your resilience to ransom?

The Bottom Line

Resilience defined as being all about mental or physical toughness can be a very strong driver within organisations, groups and teams. However, instead of enabling flexibility (which is true resilience), it encourages a resistance **towards** something, a toughening up **'in the face of'**, a push **against**. If sustained, this forcefulness leads to brittleness which in turn destroys the possibility of a truer, more flexible set of responses. Being tough can lead to burnout.

If this is one of the myths that you are attracted to, you can start to shift your thinking. Start by noticing. Being present, one of the Top Enablers of resilience, is your ticket to widening your perspective. See Chapter 9 for more on how to be present. Once you notice more, you will understand more. And that in turn will create the conditions for a more flexible response.

This is living the Resilient Way.

Chapter 2

Myth 2: Resilience Is Having More Control

'I've had to relinquish control.
I'm not frightened of the future –
you just have to trust yourself.'

Alternative view

Person 1: Knock knock.
Person 2: Who's there?
Person 1: Control Freak. Now you say,
'Control Freak who?'

Chapter Overview

This chapter will challenge your thinking on whether or not you need control.

Within your day-to-day life, you may well believe that having control is a good thing. Life, however, does not always afford you this; many things are not within your control and this can feel very uncomfortable.

This chapter sets out a different way of looking at control. Instead of a fixed view of control, it offers the Resilient Way, where control is considered alongside taking responsibility and accountability. The chapter explores the balance between control, responsibility and accountability, and how high-resilience people proactively manage how to respond to different situations.

Finally, you get the chance to review this kind of new thinking for yourself via reflective exercises.

The Resilience Scene

Google Trends shows up all sorts of interesting searches that the world is using. Google Trends is a search trends feature that shows how frequently a given search term is entered into Google's search engine relative to the site's total search volume over a given period of time. Here is what you find for the word 'control' in the twelve months from 1 May 2018 to 30 April 2019:

Google Trends Search Terms Last 12 Months: 'Control'

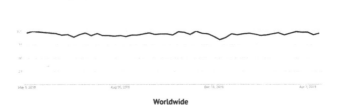

Worldwide

Source: Google Trends (https://www.google.com/trends).

The index delivered on the search term 'control' shows a near 100% use across time. That means we're searching on the term 'control' pretty much all the time – it has become normal.

In comparison to the word 'stress', 'control' seems to be much more significant:

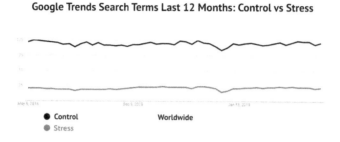

Google Trends Search Terms Last 12 Months: Control vs Stress

● Control   Worldwide
● Stress

Source: Google Trends (https://www.google.com/trends).

The word 'control' comes up in all sorts of terms beyond the concept of self-control. Often it is about placing restrictions on undesirable outcomes, such as 'crime control'. Or it's about managing risks, e.g. financial control. Self-control is the ability to restrain one's own emotions and actions and the term is included in the Google data above.

The graphs above show that there is a saturation of the concept of needing to have control; it's in everything and everywhere. It's so normal you may not even notice your drive for it. The Resilience Engine aims to bring awareness of this normalisation of the drive for control. It's a myth that you need control in every situation to feel ok, to feel safe.

(✎) **Write down**

Often we play a game at the beginning of any conference slot or with a wide audience. You can do the same right here, right now:

o Rate yourself from 1 to 10 on a 'control-freak' scale, where 10 is a total control freak and 1 is totally laid back.

   Go on, give it a go.

19

What is your score?

o   Now, rate yourself from 1 to 10 on your stress levels, where
    10 is dangerously stressed and 1 is not stressed at all.

Q Review

Compare and contrast the two scores, and how they might be
related.

With large groups, for question 1 above, we invite everyone
to stand up, and we count down from ten through to one, asking
people to sit down when it gets to their number. It is rare for
many or indeed any participants to be left standing after the
number 5; at least half and very often two thirds of any group
have sat down by the rating of 7. The same result is borne out
again and again, whether in the game above, or whether in our
media or where we seem to want control in our lives.

The Problem

The issue is that you cannot always have control.

Q Review

Consider different situations where you would prefer to have
control but just don't!

What about your team? Does each member actually deliver
what you need them to in exactly the way that you would wish?

What about your kids? Do they do what you ask them?

And yourself? Do you manage to do what your rational brain
is telling you in all situations? What about when you are about to
make a presentation and you are nervous and your mouth is dry,

you feel butterflies in your stomach, your breathing goes faster, and you feel like you're going to stutter as soon as you open your mouth. When you are forcefully telling yourself to calm down and steady yourself, to get a grip of yourself and get back into control. Does it work?

The outcomes you wish do not always come about by seeking or forcing control. Indeed, forcing control often backfires. It's the birthplace of resistance. Kids rebel, your team members resist, your own body seems to do the opposite of what you need in the moment of that presentation! What then? You might try to place control even more forcefully!

The Resilience Engine works with leaders and managers who, when experiencing a sense of lack of control, will double their efforts to gain or re-gain control. Our clients often start to manage the detail that their staff are in fact managing. Instead of creating a process of check-in and review, they as the boss covertly track emails to check up on whether things are being done. Control freakery has set in! Many organisations enforce a myriad of detailed control mechanisms on staff only to find that the reporting process has become a bureaucratic nightmare that no one respects.

Is this control? Or it is delusional thinking? The truth is, you cannot control everything. Instead of control, you might think of what will drive your confidence.

ℚ Review

What do you need to have confidence in any situation where you are not in control?

How can you set up the conditions for confidence?

Why does control come up so much in resilience?

Much of what is written and researched about resilience is researched from a deficit of resilience. This means that the resilience levels researched are at best Coping,[6] but most often are likely to be not coping, what The Resilience Engine calls Fragmentation or, lower still, near Breakdown.[6] (See Chapters 5 and 6 for a definition of these resilience levels.) Those who have a resilience level lower than Coping will seek to get back to Coping. That is a great start.

Lower levels of resilience do throw up control as an issue. Those whose resilience is lower than Coping or really long-term Coping will seek more control in order to feel safer. And feeling safe is good. So here, seeking control is helpful for your resilience.

> **Resilience is a measure of how safe you feel.**
> **The higher the resilience, the more you feel safe in your own skin, no matter what's going on.**

When you don't feel safe in your own skin, you may displace the need for safety by seeking control; having control over external things, like your diary, task list and relationships, gives a sense of stability and security.

Control freakery, when you are controlled by the need to control (!), is most often a symptom of low resilience or a long-term resilience drain. Lower resilience means that you become less resourceful, and that in turn means you can't manage to do all the things you normally do.

> **Lower resilience levels diminish your ability to access your resources, internal and external.**

22

That means you don't manage as well.
That can lead to you feeling unsafe.
That can kick in the urge to control.

At low levels of resilience, things feel like they spin out of control and so you start to hang onto anything you can control. The control-seeking is not discerning. If the urge to control is not satisfied, it will shift somewhere else. Thus the overworked nurse who can't seem to control patient flow, patient complexity and structural aspects in work, will shift to controlling everything at the dinner table with her family. Or the entrepreneur who is deeply in financial strain and worried about paying staff will seek to control some of the detailed work within his employee responsibilities, as a way of exercising the control urge.

Neither leads to a good result.

The urge to control something is often because you cannot see a way to effect control over the things that are causing you stress. So you switch to seeking control of other stuff.

The Resilient Way

The Resilient Way reframes this muddle. As awareness and understanding grow, you choose how to both influence and react.

The issue with the assumption that control is needed is two-fold:

o   When people think about being 'in control' they often get confused between controlling an internal response versus controlling external factors.

You cannot control much of what happens externally. You can influence it, but you can't control it. If you are encouraging yourself or others to 'control' external factors in your workplace, you are probably placing a completely delusional objective upon them.

You can, however, give yourself the possibility of an internal reaction that will lead to success: the Resilient Way. This starts by proactively holding an intention, which then enables a clearer choice in any moment, to react to support that intention, no matter what.

Proact to **React** intentionally

o   Being 'in control' can mean keeping a lid on your emotions. See Chapter 1, Myth 1, on what The Resilience Engine research shows about that. In a nutshell, this forced containment of your emotions leads to blind spots, resentment and ill health.

The Resilient Way is to honour the emotion that you feel, whilst not being hijacked by it. Instead you choose to react according to the intention that you hold.

The Resilient Way accounts for two other significant factors at play in any situation: responsibility and accountability.

When everything is balanced

CONTROL

ACCOUNTABILITY   RESPONSIBILITY

resilience
engine

Review

What is the relationship between these three drivers: control, responsibility and acccountability? Is it like this?

1) When control is much greater than accountability

CONTROL

ACCOUNTABILITY   RESPONSIBILITY

resilience
engine

All control, little responsibility, little accountability?

When the control you seek is out of kilter with the control needs, or the risks, of the activity itself.

Indeed, you're really all about having control for control's sake, independent of the outcome.

Example settings

At home, when you like doing things your way, e.g. baking, cooking or packing the car. You seek some kind of 'perfection'. This might be in the result itself and/or maybe in the process of feeling organised.

Exerting less control may deliver even better results – at least everyone might feel more relaxed! What's more, the results are probably good enough.

 Or is it like this?

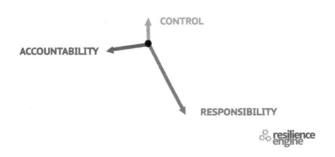

You feel the responsibility acutely, but you don't have sufficient control, and you certainly don't have accountability!

You may really care about others. You may want to make it better for them. You have an undue sense of responsibility as a result, but you cannot in fact control whether things can improve, nor have any real accountability to act on how to improve their situation.

Example settings

Caring for others when in complex situations; reactive sectors such as the NHS and the emergency services; or when you have been mentoring someone about how to deal with a situation. They are the ones to act in the situation, but you can feel very responsible for them.

 Or is it like this?

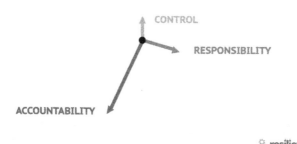

You feel all the accountability but have little of the responsibility and you can't get any control either!

Example settings
Senior Leadership, Collaborative Leadership, Project Management. Parenting!

In all of these situations, you cannot control specifics. You do not have responsibility for many of the tasks. Instead, you hold accountability for the outcomes.

All you can do is to set up appropriate levels of responsibility via others, and help them define what 'good' looks like.

Accountability is owning the bottom line, the final outcome, the final output even. You are the one that's answerable. In ethics and governance, accountability is answerability, blameworthiness, liability, and the expectation of account-giving. You owe an explanation.

Responsibility is having some part or whole ownership of a task, action or event. You aim to take care of all the elements that enable a great piece of work. You execute them with the most care you can. It does not mean having accountability. It just means carrying out your part of the task to the best of your ability. You have a duty to complete your part of the task, but someone else is accountable for the impact.

Obviously you may hold both. Most leaders are both responsible and accountable.

Control can look similar to responsibility, with one big difference. Control is related to things going your way. Indeed you will manipulate the situation to achieve your vision of what the outcome should be. It's close to perfectionism, where you are emotionally attached to the level of 'good' in the outcome. It's got to be right, your 'right'.

Learning the skills of exercising and enabling control via others is necessary for all leadership. However, if it becomes engrained that by having control you feel safer, it can become the only choice, it's the only way to feel safe.

Do you need control to feel safe?
If you don't have control, do you feel unsafe?

If you spot someone seeking control in a forceful or tense kind of way, it is not necessarily a sign that the person wants accountability and/or responsibility for what they appear to seek control over. It's most often a symptom of their resilience being lower than Coping. It can also be out of habit, formed again and again because having a sense of control helps the person feel safe. If this is part of your core driver, it leads to control freak behaviour and a real stuckness. It is also a source of negative stress.

Seeking control in every situation is the opposite to acting in the Resilient Way which seeks to engineer an appropriate and flexible response in any situation. Having and managing control is only half the equation of the resilience-control relationship. The other side of the equation is learning to be safe when you don't have control. It requires trusting.

This all relates to what Steven Covey[7] named the Circle of Influence versus the Circle of Concern, and indeed what he develops further and calls the Circle of Commitment which contains those things you commit to. Covey says:

I am not a product of my circumstances. I am a product of my decisions.

Things in your Circle of Influence are just that, things you can directly influence. Things in your Circle of Commitment are those that you decide you can and will influence. Things in your Circle of Concern are out of your influence. You may care about them to some extent, but you cannot influence them.

Energy spent in matters outside of your influence, ie those in your Circle of Concern, diminishes the energy you could put into those things that you can influence, ie those things in your Circle of Influence. You become less effective in the areas you can affect. You achieve less, and you shift to a reactive, victim mode.

The findings of The Resilience Engine research show an interesting relationship between resilience and control. Those with the highest resilience will take accountability, responsibility and indeed, where appropriate, control for the things that are meaningful for them, **where they can enact control**. But they let go of where they don't need or indeed can't control.

Being in control is not needed to be resilient.
Taking responsibility and, as appropriate, taking accountability are needed to be resilient.

Seeking to advance the things that matter to you is good where you have accountability and responsibility. It's where you have the possibility of holding a proactive set of intentions. This is what Covey[7] calls your Circle of Influence; focussing here increases your resilience.

In a lower resilience state, you can easily be distracted by items that concern you, but over which you have little influence. Any tiredness can exaggerate this tendency. Energy spent in these matters leads to a contraction of your Circle of Influence and that leads to a dropping of your resilience. A drop you cannot afford because your resilience is already under threat.

Understanding your own levels of resilience is critical for understanding how you might be reacting. If you find yourself beholden to matters outwith your concern, it's likely your resilience level is low. Accepting this allows you to shift away from this wasted effort towards taking responsibility for what you can affect.

Overall, the Resilient Way is to set up the conditions for a 'good' result. This will include not just the 'what' of the task, but also the 'why', 'when', 'how', 'how often', 'how much', 'who', plus the learning process to ensure that any plan is adjusted appropriately to account for new data and insight into the situation. The Resilient Way ensures that responsibilities are clear and agreed amongst everyone involved, and accountability is with the right people and is being enacted.

To trust that you can enable this in others in the first place means you need firstly to trust that you can live the Resilient Way.

At the start, the Resilient Way can be demanding. You need to be clear. You need to be enabling. You need to be aware of assumptions. You need to be open to your own intentions and those of others. As experience builds, however, if the Resilient Way becomes part of our capability, it's a gateway to having higher capacity, feeling at ease, and not suffering from the negative stress reaction. All good!

Overall, the Resilient Way will give you confidence in you and your team's ability to deliver, whilst loosening the need for control. That saves a whole lot of anxiety and stress, plus it releases capacity in everyone.

Applying the Resilient Way

Identifying and owning what you can in fact influence

© The Resilience Engine 2019

Take some time to consider how you spend your time. It will include doing, thinking, analysing. And it will include moaning and resenting!

(✐) **Write down**

In two columns capture things that are in your influence, and those things that you can't influence.

Consider how much time you spend on each side. You may choose to do this precisely using hours, or more generally using days. You may choose indeed to apply percentages. Whichever you choose, do this honestly!

It will look something like this.

	Can Influence (Circle of Influence)	Can't Influence (Circle of Concern)
Doing		
	Time Total:	Time Total:
Thinking/ Analysing		
	Time Total:	Time Total:
Moaning/ Resenting		
	Time Total:	Time Total:

🔍 Review

How much time do you spend in areas that you can influence? How much time do you spend in areas that you cannot influence? What insights do you get when looking at the ratio between these?

⇢ Change

What would you like to drop that is draining your energies? What would you like to do more of?

✔ Commit

What will you really commit to? This could be just one or two things.

Remember to focus on things that matter to you, and that you can influence.

Stories of Resilience

A client of The Resilience Engine who attended one of our Being Resilient workshops asked me a question:

I have always needed to control things in my life. But how do you manage, when you have to manage other people? You can't control how they are. What do you do?

My response at the time came from a deep-rooted sense of this client not taking responsibility for her own needs and behaviour. I got the sense that she was shifting the responsibility towards me so I could tell her how to feel safe. I replied with this in mind by asking her:

Do you know how you feel safe?
For example what do you need to feel secure in delivery of anything at work?

The question was confusing for her. But it got inside her head: she looked puzzled but engaged. At the break she came up to me and again the same question:

But how do you manage, when you have to manage other people? I am stressed all the time because I can't control how they are. What should I do?

I replied:

This is related to trusting. Trusting yourself first and foremost. Then to trusting others. What's it like to trust yourself?

She looked at me again puzzled, but I could see she was definitely working on it. Later the same day, the group were doing an exercise on learning, designed to help each participant experience how they learn and in particular to experience how learning shortcuts can backfire. (See Chapter 9 for more on the Top Enablers of resilience.) This client got her 'Aha!' moment in the middle of this exercise as she explained to me immediately afterwards:

I have got it!

I am always in the plan-do-plan-do and often in the do-do-do areas of learning. It's because I am trying to control it all, I end up doing so much. Then I'm caught just there, do-do-do. Whilst I am there, I am not looking at the actual output of anything – I am not looking to see what has actually happened. I am not thinking! That's what I need to do. I know I trust myself and others if I can look at the outcome of what is happening, and seeking to understand whether that is any good or not, and if not, adjust things. It's entirely different than seeking to control. Thank you!

The client went away quite different. What a turnaround in perspective in just one day! I wondered where this new insight would take her, and in which areas of her work and indeed personal life she might end up feeling not just less stressed and more at ease, but indeed more successful as a result!

☺ The Resilience Lens
This story may resonate with you.

How often do you ignore looking at the actual results of a task/project because you're so caught up controlling?

How much do you take responsibility for the challenges you face?

What, if anything, would you like to change in your relationship with control?

The Bottom Line

This chapter has been all about busting the myth that you need control to be resilient. You do not.

Those with the highest resilience take responsibility, accountability as appropriate, and control only where it is necessary. The Resilient Way is to enable others through meaningful control mechanisms that bring success. Then let go control of everything else.

Be clear on what you are accountable for. Be clear on what you have responsibility for. Decide if you need to exercise control over any of this, and if you don't, ensure that the conditions for success are agreed.

Then leave people to get on with it whilst you get on with what you need to do.

Chapter 3

Myth 3:
You Need Confidence
for Resilience

*'They danced my dance,
I didn't have the confidence to
portray the negative side.'*

'Reassurance is ineffective.'

Chapter Overview

This chapter sets out to show that the myth that confidence is needed for resilience is over-simplistic.

The chapter is based on The Resilience Engine's research and practice of ten years. It is not a treatise on what confidence is or how to build it in all contexts. Whilst our research draws on the academic research on confidence that exists in psychology, clinical research and child development, our own resilience research findings and practice is with leaders and managers in the workplace. Leaders and managers, by dint of actually having a job and being successful enough to keep it (even if sometimes there are wobbles), are by their nature mostly 'functioning' as opposed to not functioning. 'Not functioning' gets a lot of research attention and this naturally skews the evidence base towards where there is a deficit of resilience.

The Resilience Engine's research contributes to the debate on how confidence and resilience relate. So it is that we offer three core insights into understanding:

o How resilience underpins self-efficacy,[8–12] the confidence to succeed in a particular domain or accomplish a task. Here resilience is an input.

o How secure bases[13] are drawn on, extended and indeed created through a Resilient Way of living. The idea of secure bases as people comes from Attachment Theory,[14–16] but has been extended in research to include not just people. George Kohlrieser defines these in *Care to Dare*[13] as

a person, place, goal, or object that provides a sense of protection, safety, and caring and offers a source of inspiration and energy to explore, take risks, and seek challenge.

A sense of safety is the same as resilience. The relationship between resilience and confidence is two-way: secure bases deliver resilience as an outcome, and in the living of resilience, secure bases are supported, extended and created. We describe the relationship with secure bases and resilience as a 'Generative Loop' based on learning.

o How resilience underpins the confidence you have in navigating future challenges. Resilience here acts as an input.

So resilience acts as both an input into and an output of confidence.

The Resilience Scene

Much of the academic and popular management literature states that for resilience you need confidence: *'Self confidence is a crucial component of resilience because it creates a forward motion of positivity and optimism.'*[17] Many resilience evaluation methods[18-21] use confidence as a survey measure contributing to your output resilience level. The voice of this body of literature has resilience as an output of confidence. A few writers and some researchers don't try to distinguish one from the other and instead just conflate the two concepts. Resilience is confidence, confidence is resilience.

Carol Dweck's work[22] illustrates it's more about protecting the fragility of confidence. Indeed she says that in the growth mindset, which is very aligned to resilience, *'you don't always need confidence';* in Dweck's book, effort is the key to achievement which in turn brings confidence.

Which comes first then, confidence or resilience?

The Problem

There are three problems with this myth of resilience.

Problem 1: The assumed definition of confidence

The word confidence is often used without being clear what it actually means. There are many levels of confidence. John Leary Joyce, a psychologist and Chair of the Academy of Executive Coaching, refers to four levels of mental states:

> *Self-Hatred where there is no resilience; Self-Doubt where there is an inner critical voice that is destructive; Self-Belief, and finally Self-Esteem where there is true compassion.*[23]

There are also different forms of confidence:

Self-efficacy
Courage and determination

Self-actualisation
Being in flow[1,2]
Self-acceptance
And I'm sure many more!

The type and level of confidence needed for resilience is unclear. Can you be a little bit confident and still manage to cope? If you lose your confidence in your ability to execute a task or project, does that mean you lose your resilience only in that context or in others also?

Self-confidence does not mean believing that you will 'succeed'. At least not according to external measures of success. For example, I play tennis and am an avid amateur. But I rarely succeed according to the league in my tennis club! But I play well enough for what I look for – it's a real success for me. Here's why:

o   I love the exercise.
o   I love the competitive element with myself and others which unlocks joy in me.
o   This is a free space for the speed that I like to go at. In work if I go at the pace I'd like to, I just cause chaos!
o   I feel immensely satisfied with the occasional winning shot.
o   I love the straightforward camaraderie, and that I don't have to account for any other part of myself other than I am here, right now, and am here to play.
o   I love the switching off from everything else; a singular focus for more than an hour. What a treat.
o   I love the learning. There is no doubt that in one year I have improved not just theoretically but in action.
o   And, finally, one of the best: being in the fresh air. Alive!

So I am quite confident already when I play tennis. I trust in the outcomes I am going to get. The only thing that gets in the way is if I'm tired and don't fulfil some of that energy release.

I am also immensely confident of my ability to learn. So once I get to a particular external success level, say winning more matches, I know I can learn to stabilise this. And then again if I 'improve', I can continue to extend my practice and be more a skilled tennis player.

Overall I have confidence in knowing what I get from tennis, knowing how to get this, and knowing that I can continue to get it.

Problem 2: The assumed definition of resilience

Most definitions of resilience talk about recovering from challenge or adversity. This is because most of the research has been in clinical settings where someone has suffered trauma.[24] Our cultural definitions, whether organisational culture or popular culture, also have this definition. (See Chapter 5 for more.)

Perhaps you have suffered a really difficult challenge in work, and had to recover. Your confidence during the challenge was probably mixed – maybe you knew you were 'ok' deep down, but that this particular challenge really knocked you. If you have a mixed or even muddled sense of your confidence, the implication of this myth is that your resilience will be mixed also. But in the middle of a confidence knock, you may really dig deep and drive out a much higher level of resilience, the opposite of what the myth says!

What if you face an unexpected drop in confidence suddenly? It can happen after a long stint of only just managing to cope, where any additional load feels like it would break you. Confidence is now rock bottom – is it therefore time to hang up the towel because your resilience will also be at rock bottom? That won't deliver high performance!

The mass of clinical research that exists on recovery from trauma gives rise to the singular notion of resilience that it's about recovery. Bounceback becomes a kind of destination. Bounceback is, however, not the highest level of performance, due to the cost of recovery. It's a reactive way of working and living, gearing yourself up all the time for the next challenge. There is little room for a creative, innovative set of responses. And there is little room for feeling at ease.

This definition of resilience is too limited.

Problem 3: This myth does not match all the research

Research that focusses on resilience and high performance shows something quite different from this myth:

o   The Resilience Engine's research shows a deep difference with the idea of confidence being needed for resilience.[23]

Many of the leaders described their confidence as *shaky*. For example, in their own ability within their organisation to compete. Or that they believed in their own judgement, but were not at all confident about how to influence others of the value of that judgement.

Yet these leaders demonstrated real adaptability, persistence in the face of challenge, an immense learning capability and so on. All these elements are shown in The Resilience Engine research as components of resilience. Confidence builds the more these components come together in an integrated way.

For many leaders, confidence is an outcome of resilience, not the other way around.

o Confidence comes only when you are tested, and you learn how to get through each challenge.

In sports, athletes train hard, and are tested along the way all the time. Olympic athletes will ensure their four-year training programme has plenty of world-class competitions which test their resilience: *'Regarding challenge appraisal, the world's best athletes tended to perceive stressors as opportunities for growth, development and mastery, particularly at the peak of their sporting careers.'* [24]

This is completely in line with Carol Dweck's concept of the Growth Mindset[22] which is very aligned to the Resilient Way. The Growth Mindset is underpinned wholly by learning and by the belief that your intelligence can adapt and extend if you take risks and apply effort. It also accounts for where you are more likely to succeed; that effort is only worthwhile when it is genuinely meaningful for you. According to Dweck, learning something that is genuinely motivating is key for high performance.

o Within the business schools across the world, leadership confidence is a core part of research activities. Literature on leadership, whether from IMD, Harvard Business School or the like, tells us that an underlying confidence contributes to resilience. This underlying confidence enables authentic leadership, what George Kohlrieser calls 'Secure Base Leadership'.[13]

The research on high performance and resilience gives both ideas, that resilience is driven by confidence and confidence driven by resilience. Both are inputs, both are outputs.

Rosabeth Moss Kanter of Harvard Business School, who specialises in strategy, innovation and leadership talks about the cornerstones of confidence as accountability, collaboration, and initiative.[25,26] Indeed she implies that self-belief comes from some of the core components of resilience. She says high performers

- *can put troubles in perspective because they are ready for them.* This is getting perspective, part of the Adaptive Capacity[23] of resilience.
- *rehearse through diligent practice and preparation.* This is based on the learning cycle, one of the Top Enablers of resilience.
- *put facts on the table and review what went right or wrong in the last round, in order to shore up strengths and pinpoint weaknesses and to encourage personal responsibility for actions.* Again this is learning, and especially looking at the resilience data. (See Chapters 5 and 9 for more information.)
- *stress collaboration and teamwork – a common goal.* Purpose is a core enabler of resilience.
- *seek creative ideas for improvement and innovation.* This is releasing surplus energy, and aligning learning towards purpose, all core enablers of resilience.

All these resilience factors combine to give the outcome of confidence.

Other areas of research also show confidence as an outcome of resilience. Resilience contributes to confidence by demonstrating what you can achieve even in challenging circumstances, as this extract from 'The confidence to know I can survive: Resilience and recovery in post-quake Christchurch'[27] shows:

> *For some women, like Raewyn Iketau, telling their earthquake stories intensified their sense of how resourceful and innovative they had been. Narrating their stories was a dynamic way of recognising their confidence, their capacity for survival, their usefulness to others and the strength of their social networks.*

With these multiple sources of research, you see that confidence and resilience do not have a one-way relationship, but instead are interlocked and generative together.

The Resilient Way

The original Resilience Engine research illustrates that you need self-acceptance, not self-esteem or even self-belief, to be resilient. You need a deep self-acceptance of

Your own power and voice
Where you get hooked or held hostage
What you need and don't need
Where you do not have strong ability
You in relation to others

Self-acceptance is at the heart of personal resilience, and is enabled massively in the Top Enabler 'being present'. Other Resilience Engine[23] factors that deliver confidence come into play. The big ticket items are set out in Chapters 5, 7 and 9. They can be summarised as follows:

o   Setting boundaries for safety
o   Maximising your energies, so you can act successfully on the meaningful things in your life
o   Learning, learning, learning. And as part of that, forgiving yourself and others when you or they mess up.

In the living of resilience, confidence flows. The Resilience Engine sees the relationship between confidence and resilience as a generative loop:

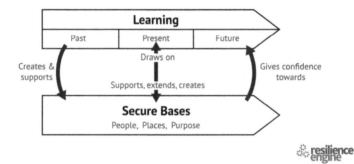

Resilience and Confidence "The Generative Loop"

Secure bases can be drawn on in the moment of any situation, by bringing them into your attention, your memory, or indeed how you feel. They give you a lift, a burst of energy, inspiration to keep going or to look about for other options, or to shift towards something more meaningful.

Knowing that these secure bases work for real for you in your day-to-day work and life is what delivers confidence in your future.

Many of The Resilience Engine coaching clients return to an early secure base they have neglected. For example, horse-riding, or a sport. In doing so they find their whole life transformed, they feel good, they feel happy they are investing in themselves, and the return they get from doing so is immense.

One of the simplest ways to enhance a secure base of place is to go to that place often. So it is, say, with your favourite mountain or beach. Or a favourite part of your town or city. This place offers you peace, calm, energy, a sense of being able just to 'be present'. And at the same time, in that being present, it offers you connection with what is possible.

By going often to this place you bring everything of yourself to it, all your successes and your joys, plus all your fears and worries. You are whole in this place. And it's because of being able to be whole, you don't have to prove anything. It is this 'being present' which is one of the key enablers of resilience, and it affords you the courage of seeing new ways.

If you're lucky, educated and have a great family, you will have a strong set of secure bases. If you do not, you need to build these bases.

The Resilient Way contributes to, enhances and indeed creates secure bases:

o The learning from your past experiences contributes to how your secure bases support you and give you safety.
o Difficulties of previous relationships, where maybe your boundaries were badly managed, will help you understand which people now really can and do act as a secure base for you.

o   Challenges that you have overcome will enhance your sense
    of purpose or meaning today and in the future.
o   When you do come through a period that is tough, you
    realise how important your secure bases are to you. And that
    enhances your level of security in what you're about in this
    world.
o   New meaning in your life, whether new places, new
    relationships or new purpose, all can form new secure
    bases.

Living in a more Resilient Way in the present enhances your
secure bases. The more you invest in your relationship with these
secure bases, the more they provide that sense of both security
and inspiration to take risks.

Your secure bases plus your ability to learn give you a
platform for going forward confidently. These two factors are the
'killer' components of confidence.

You know that you can adapt as appropriate. You know that
the way ahead will feel more coherent with regard to who you
are. You know that whatever challenges are ahead you can count
on your resilience, and even if all goes belly up, your secure bases
will still be there.

This combination delivers tremendous confidence. It is
the stuff of what The Resilience Engine calls Breakthrough[6]
resilience, a level where you are resilient no matter what is
going on. It's where you are most adaptable, energised and
persistent in your goals. It is where high performance and
wellbeing are entirely synergistic. See Chapter 5 for further
details.

Applying the Resilient Way

Secure bases

© The Resilience Engine 2019

 Review

What are your secure bases? Include all the people, places, purposes, events, activities etc that provide you with both a sense of security and inspiration.

How often do you invest in each of these?

Which are the most straightforward for you in your life?

Which might be complex? (Often relationships fall into this.)

 Change

How might you draw on all your secure bases more?

For those secure bases that you find complex, how might you make them simpler and more accessible to you?

 Commit

Invest specifically in your most important secure bases.

Learning

(See Chapter 9 for more on this Top Enabler of resilience.)

© The Resilience Engine 2019

 Review

If you have sufficient capacity for learning (ie not overwhelmed by things you are having to cope with, or just fatigued because

49

of being so busy) look at your barriers to resilience with the help of Chapter 7.

Reflect on the underlying causes of these barriers.

When you are held back by something that is a fear or doubt, this undermines your resilience and therefore your confidence. Fear is born often from interrupting the necessary learning about something in the past.

⇦ Change

What do you need to learn in order to let go of, or move on from, issues in your past?

✔ Commit

Accept the truth about your own fears and doubts. Being able to be vulnerable is resilience enhancing, and therefore confidence enhancing.

Stories of Resilience

Vincent

Vincent is a senior leader within his company and is trusted by the CEO. He is used to feeling successful: he is evidentially capable and he likes to control things to be the way he wants. He's not a control freak by any means, but he does like to be able to dictate quickly and clearly how things go within any situation. This has brought him great success. Since he likes being successful he keeps exercising this same leadership style.

He has been recently tasked to set up and manage indirect channels with a new set of franchisees. The aim is to extend the company's selling capability without increasing its employee base. Franchisees have passed a rigorous set of criteria and interview, understand the company's services and have the capability of selling and delivering them. The company's services are high end and high touch; they are people oriented and are delivered with a great level of integrity. Each franchisee is expected to apply the company values of respect and integrity to everything they do.

Dealing with the franchisees is challenging. Vincent believes he excels in how this kind of model should work. He thinks that the franchisees, although actively competitive in the marketplace, will come together to share best practice and learn together, and this will give the company an edge. However, whilst they are supposed to be both collaborative and competitive, they are in fact suffering from a lot of tension.

Franchisees are moaning about favouritism in terms of support, and who gets given the tip-off about certain contracts. They don't understand how the regional patches are carved up, nor how they can actually compete with the company's direct channels. A number of them complain and Vincent keeps having to go back as to why things have been set up the way they have. He finds himself on the defensive and this is extremely irritating for him, since in fact he just wants to go out and win new business.

Vincent has a run-in with one franchisee who was bypassed for a particular deal despite being best placed geographically to deliver on it; another franchisee was automatically awarded the contract. Vincent is forthright in telling the ignored franchisee that he and clients needed more confidence in them before directly assigning any contract work. The franchisee, relatively new to the whole model and still finding their feet, leaves the conversation annoyed, deflated and in fact with a strong sense of lack of trust. They thought that the company was supposed to act with integrity! What happened to trust? The franchisee is left questioning the value of staying with the company.

Vincent is left feeling annoyed and still under pressure. This franchisee is barking up the wrong tree: instead of whinging about not getting a particular contract, they should be going out and winning new business! Indeed Vincent's confidence in being able to make this whole thing work is dropping. Why can't these new channels just get on with the way of working he has set up, and get out and do the business?! Why are they needing so much hand-holding?

The Resilience Lens

Vincent's resilience is normally at Bounceback[6] levels. He likes challenges, he seeks them and enjoys performing in them. But he forgets that in the middle of a challenge he can find it difficult and that his behaviour becomes rigid and dominating.

This particular situation of a new and difficult indirect team of franchisees, and the model of operation that has been set up for both competition and collaboration, has all sorts of unintended consequences. Vincent cannot put his hands around it all. Some franchisees are new to the whole idea and model, and despite Vincent explaining it, still don't understand how to operate within it; they would rather have a straightforward collaborative partnership model. Despite Vincent trying to get control, he is failing, and each discussion around the business model is draining his confidence.

His position during the conversation with the bypassed franchisee is one of 'fight', a stress reaction. Vincent is impatient, is feeling under the cosh, and the stress leads to him being blunt and indeed unkind. Instead of being flexible in his response he becomes the opposite: dogged and dominant. The consequence of the tension he holds as a result is that he treats the franchisee arrogantly.

Vincent needs to accept the reality of the pressure he faces, and allow himself to rest, to get help, and to learn to be present to the franchisee's concerns more. If he doesn't he is in danger of losing them, and that in itself would put his leadership of the whole initiative in question.

The Resilience Lens

Who are you drawn to more in this story, Vincent or the franchisee?

What happens to you when you feel under pressure and your confidence is slipping? Do you allow yourself to step back and invest in getting a breather and more perspective? Or do you bash on?

What would you advise Vincent to do?

The Bottom Line

Confidence and resilience are synergistic. The two killer components for confidence are having a living, active set of secure bases, plus being able to learn. The relationship between confidence and resilience can be described by the Generative Learning Loop, where each contributes to the other.

o Learning is at the heart of resilience. Learning from past experiences delivers self-efficacy for the future.

o Secures bases are drawn on and fed by resilience thinking. These give a deep sense of both security and inspiration to take risks in life.

Embracing both is part of the Resilient Way.

Chapter 4

Myth 4:
Driving Efficiency Delivers
the Highest Productivity

'The impact of lack of resilience is ineffectiveness.
Other aspects include innovation, creativity.
This in survival mode is the first thing to go.'

Chapter Overview

This chapter sets out why chasing down efficiency to the n'th degree is wasted effort. Whilst removing the obviously inefficient aspects is necessary for the result to be good, trying to endlessly improve efficiency will not deliver a benefit.

Once major inefficiencies are removed from any given task, any productivity gain is made via an investment in resilience.

The Resilience Scene

Hear ye, hear ye, hear ye!

List-makers
Busy managers and leaders
Productivity specialists
Process improvement consultants
Quality seekers
Lean process experts

All juggling mums and dads
And all and anyone who seek the enlightened way of efficiency
Hear ye, hear ye, hear ye!

You are the experts of process. You are the experts of efficiency. You aim for smooth operations. You aim to prioritise clearly, assign resources, run the machine, analyse the results, improve the results, eke out another drop of productivity, whilst reducing costs and increasing the output of the task.

Task 1. Done.
Task 2. Done.
Task 3. Done.
Next, Task 4.
Then, Tasks 5, 6, 7…

All this at reasonable quality. You are good at ensuring the balance of efficiency versus sufficient quality to meet the needs of the customer or process.

You make lists to get organised. You make other lists to ensure what is important and what is not important. You identify plans, measures of success, and key processes to manage all the tasks.

You aim for efficiency big time.

The Problem

Driving for efficiency is hard. It's time-consuming. It's a full-time job just to stand still. The demands in the workplace are increasing: you are asked to do more with less, including leading through complexity.

The first step you get into is to get real about inefficiency. You iron out obvious inefficiencies in any system to ensure a smooth enough operation. Inefficiencies within any process are costly in real terms, and indeed to your resilience.

The issue is that tackling inefficiency takes a whole lot of capacity. And if you haven't got the time, you don't manage this well. How many times have you sensed that someone else is doing part of your job, or you are doing part of someone else's? You know there is duplication. But neither of you have the whole picture, so you keep going and hope that maybe you will join up at some point soon, so you can sort it all out.

Consider your own efficiency.

Take your process for getting out each morning to work. You will have worked out the most efficient – the least resistant, smoothest – method to do what you need to do and exit, intact (!), with keys and phone in hand, appropriately dressed, clean and fed, as you need for the day. And if you include in your system your family, you might include how best to get the kids washed, dressed, fed and equipped with everything they need for the day also. During normal working days, you are probably aiming to do all of this within the minimum time.

But sometimes there is a spanner in the works! The negative stress reaction kicks in when...

you don't find your keys or phone

one of your kids announces they need money/different lunch/costume/signed sheet/whatever for something at school

you overslept so you're late.

The impact of that first inefficiency or interrupt can be layers upon layers:

> More traffic on the road later now means you'll be late for your client, and that will have a knock-on effect across the whole day.

> Late arrival means not feeling prepared for that first meeting, and you may get nervy in the middle of it, and take your frustrations out on the team, who will in turn have their tails down and slink off from the meeting demotivated and annoyed.

> You lose perspective more easily and so the small drama mid-morning becomes a big drama! You handle it all quite inefficiently so it just ends up as a big pile of rubbish you now need to deal with. Feeling like things are spiralling out of control, you then seek to control whatever you can and you lose that spark of innovation you needed to solve that difficult problem X which has been sitting on your desk for ages. The morning routine has blown that possibility; you have no choice other than to leave it for another day. The 'difficult' pile grows.

The results of all this include the stress reaction on your body. All that adrenalin and cortisol running around your system, depleting your immunity system and leaving you open to health issues. If this builds, it can lead to serious long-term negative stress. (See Chapter 7, 'More Resilience = Less Stress'.)

Your own inefficiency definitely merits attention but in this layering up towards negative stress, your wellbeing deserves your attention more.

Driving out inefficiency takes you only so far. There are three issues with a singular focus on inefficiency:

o How can you maintain a super-man or super-woman level of effort on this all the time?

   Efficiency-chasing creates a burden. Whilst productivity improves a little, you become a slave to efficiency. That creates demotivation. That in turn then means that hard-earned productivity gains are short-lived and things slip backwards.

o Once you have an efficient process for it all, but you still don't have enough time to do everything, what then?

   An option often sought as a short-term solution is to increase the work hours. You drop non-vital activities. You don't go out so much with your friends maybe. You don't play the sport you normally do but instead cut the time down to just going to the gym which you enjoy less, but at least you're doing something! You get up earlier so you can fit more in. You are determined not to drop any balls. However, the juggling causes fatigue. Over time, you forget what it's like to feel any different. Being tired and juggling and feeling like you're not making much headway becomes the new norm.

o Lastly, and important for leadership, what about time for strategic thinking, innovation and space for creativity? If you spend all your time focussing on the efficiency of all your processes, there is no room for free-wheeling and being imaginative. Being able to have the freedom for creative thinking is important. An all-efficient person is definitely not a creative one!

When trying to be efficient has got the better of you

At a certain stage, the drive for efficiency dries up and instead you start to shift your focus to achieving more balance. You shift from this state of over-juggling and feeling tired, to your inner needs, such as rest, sleep, exercise, time out of work. You strive for work–life balance.

The term was coined in the 1970s/80s[28] and introduced the concept of an efficient use of time between the main contexts in which you operate so that your time allocation is stricter between the core areas of your life. Work–life balance is often the domain of New Year resolutions, full of promise but often tricky to follow through on.

> You **say** you'll set working hours more strictly to get home earlier, but you end up putting work in your bag and sneaking it in at weekends or later in the evening.

> You **say** you'll spend three slots of 1–2 hours per week on exercise, to invest in your health properly. You find it takes too much willpower; willpower needs energy which you just don't have.

> You **say** you're going to get up earlier every day so you can go out for a walk with the dog, giving you fresh air and much needed exercise, without compromising work or home time. But this eats into your sleep so you're more and more tired as the time goes on, making you a lot less efficient in the way you tackle all the tasks you have to do each week. Efficiency has gone out of the window!

The blurring of the start and finish of the working day due to the prevalence of technology and the internet makes it an even more fuzzy concept. Work–life balance. What a lovely idea but not quite so in practice.

Your own concept of what makes you feel in balance will be completely different from another reader's. Following general advice therefore won't work for you. Certainly what won't work is the idea of cleanly deciding on a specific amount of time for work, and a specific amount of time for personal interests and health.

Dan Thurmon is an author and keynote speaker on balance, or rather, how you need to be *Off Balance On Purpose*.[29] Dan talks about how you can never achieve the perfect balance. He offers the idea of five spheres that need to be connected with what he calls 'lifelines'. The five spheres are:

Work
Relationships
Health
Spirit
Interests.

He says that the idea that you can keep the time dedicated to any of the spheres really clean is nonsense because the five spheres of life are *'constantly interacting with your thinking, in your mind'*. So there can't be a true demarcation between them.

So what will work? How can you get the capacity you need?!

The Resilient Way

If you have ironed out the obvious inefficiencies, the real upsurge in productivity comes from resilience. With resilience you can double your capacity:

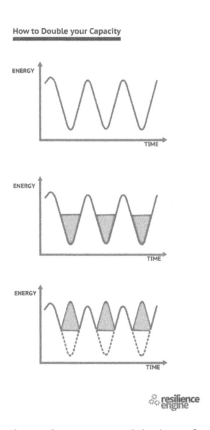

How to Double your Capacity

The diagram above shows a typical high performer's energy, which goes up during times of challenge, and down in the aftermath. This is a 'Bounceback' level of resilience, and shows that whilst the person gets through the challenge, there is a cost in energy terms. In the downs of the aftermath, not only is this a loss of capacity, it is also where the most inefficiencies reside. To be clear, you are most inefficient when you are tired.

The Resilient Way reverses the 'downs', which leads to the doubling of your capacity. Imagine!

The high performer does this by investing in their Adaptive Capacity,[23] the component of resilience that gives access to the real flexibility day to day. Other elements give you stability, but this is the big one for releasing capacity to do the stuff you love.

Those with the highest resilience invest, in a normal period, 35% of their time to what The Resilience Engine calls 'Adaptive Capacity'.

Your Adaptive Capacity is the fuel in your resilience tank – it gets used up day to day, and you need to keep replenishing it. For the highest level of resilience, you need to allocate that 35% of your time. It's a huge allocation.

You will get more capacity as a result. You will be more productive. And you will be able to maintain that level of high efficiency, for the times you need to, and then free-wheel all the way for the times you want to be creative, blob, be silly and have fun.

Your Adaptive Capacity is made up of three main components:

o   Firstly, perspective – the ability to grasp context. Being able to step back from a situation in order to better see and understand. This implies an ability to weigh up a range of factors, from how very different groups of people will interpret a gesture, to being able to put a single interaction or one bit of information in perspective.

o   The second is refreshing yourself. Consider this as energy, the combination of physical, emotional, mental and spiritual energy. Energy is directly proportional to resilience; they follow the same ups and downs. Whilst not the same, energy is a major component of resilience. Those with the highest resilience will invest in their energy on a very regular basis, not just to keep it at neutral at the end of the day, but to give surplus. See more in Chapter 9, 'Top Enablers of Resilience'.

o   The last component is pacing yourself. It's an advanced skill whereby you manage your load according to your capacity on a continuous basis. It's like a souped-up version of the learning cycle[30–32] which allows you to see what is coming down the line, and smooth out bumps before they arise. (See Chapter 9, 'Top Enablers of Resilience' for more information).

Tony Wong,[33] a productivity specialist, talks about the following areas:

o   halving your to-do list
o   taking more breaks
o   starting your day with a good breakfast and either some mindfulness or exercise so that you're set up with energy for the day ahead
o   making sure you have perspective on what matters to you from the get-go in the morning so that your priorities are not hijacked by others' demands
o   managing when you do the most challenging items on your to-do list to be in line with when you have the highest energy
o   being truthful with how you spend your time, and whether this is on the priority items or just faffing
o   doing one thing at a time.

> These are all about pacing, perspective and energy. The specific items from Tony Wong may not work for you personally, but they start to illustrate what these three elements within the Adaptive Capacity can mean in application day to day. See Chapter 9, 'Top Enablers of Resilience', for more.

How does resilience release capacity?

- ○ You get rid of unnecessary resilience drains.
- ○ You see options more readily and often in easier, faster ways.
- ○ You have fewer iterations in any task to achieve 'good'.
- ○ You stop sweating the detail.
- ○ You don't seek to resolve things that are unresolvable. You don't keep going and going at something when it won't budge. You accept it, and move away until the issue has altered or diminished in some way, or you are more resourced to tackle it.
- ○ You pull in extra resources as required.
- ○ You learn. This really is the key to it all. You learn, learn, learn. And that means you can go forward more resourcefully.

Applying the Resilient Way

Your Adaptive Capacity

© The Resilience Engine 2019

 **Write down**

Write down for each element of your own Adaptive Capacity both how you support this and what you do that drains it. Here's my current example which highlights a distinct lack of focus on pacing, causing an unnecessary resilience drain:

Adaptive Capacity Element	Supportive	Unsupportive
Getting Perspective	Weekly calls to colleagues outside of main team, just to sense check what is going on Switching off mobile data at weekend	Being over-busy Allowing stress to get the better of me
Refreshing Yourself	Tennis Family time Sleep Stopped drinking during week	Being over-busy Saying yes to new things when I haven't finished old ones
Pacing	Very little! Note this means I really have a gap in my Adaptive Capacity!	No planning!

🔍 Review

Which areas of your Adaptive Capacity are you happy with? Which areas are you less happy with?
What resources are available to you – either internal or external – that could help?

⇦ Change

With the Resilient Way you answer the following questions honestly:

- o Is this resilience-boosting? (Or resilience-draining?)
  - What is actually meaningful to you? Meaning will give you energy.
  - If it's not meaningful, how can you either shift it or let it go?
  - If you can't shift it or let it go, what is the optimal quality/effort ratio?

- o What are the criteria for 'good'?
  - What level of quality is needed here?
  - When does it need to be done by?
  - How long realistically will this take?
  - Who else needs to know/have input into this?

- o What do you actually have capacity for? And how can you align your/others' capacity to meet everything on your plate realistically?
  - What is your energy like right now?
  - How resourceful do you feel?
  - Who or what else can help to reduce the load?
  - What flexibility is there in the task?

- o How can you get more perspective on this matter?

Commit

Where is the most important opportunity for investment in your Adaptive Capacity? Within this, what outcome(s) do you wish for yourself?

What do you need in order to commit to making this opportunity real?

Stories of Resilience

I read a case study once during my MBA which made me stop. It was about the head of a refinery that led the most efficient plant in his organisation. The case study called him MacGregor.[34] It got the class's attention, and twenty years on the class still talks about it. Why? Because MacGregor seemed to be not just a great leader who ran one of the best plants in his organisation, his team admired him enormously, and most amazing of all, he took time off to play golf! We all wanted to be like this executive but had no idea how.

MacGregor's view

I don't make their [his subordinates'] *decision for them, and I just don't believe in participating in the decision they should be making either. We hold the weekly meeting so that I can keep informed on what they're doing and how... I used to make all the operating decisions myself, but I quit doing that a few years ago when I discovered my golf game was going to hell because I didn't have enough time to practice. Now that I've quit making other people's decisions, my game is back where it should be.*

His subordinate's view

He asked me to state precisely what the problem was... then he asked what the conditions for its solutions were. I didn't know what he meant by that question. His response was 'If you don't know what conditions have to be satisfied for a solution to be reached, how do you know when you've solved the problem?' I told him I'd never thought of approaching a problem that way and he replied, 'Then you'd better start. I'll work through this one with you this time, but don't expect me to do your problem solving for you because that's your job, not mine.'

MacGregor had the best team, and talented senior managers competed strongly to get into it. Why? What did all of this style lead to?

o   Firstly, each of his subordinates became very self-sufficient, confident, and able to handle everyone's problems. By the time they had done a good stint with MacGregor, they were ready to run their own refineries.

o   MacGregor spent much of his own time figuring out exactly how to increase the capacity of his refinery, so that any sudden demand or change could be catered for. He understood specifically the manpower and equipment needed for five different levels of production, each across different time intervals. Given the level of capital spend to increase production, and the terrible expense if the cost parameters were incorrect, he worked really hard to plan these levels out. He accounted for external and internal drivers. This is what he saw as his job, strategic planning. All the operations were left to his people.

☉ The Resilience Lens

What aspects of MacGregor do you most admire?

How clear are you on your role as a leader of the team?

How distinctive is your contribution versus that of your team?

How distinctive is each team member's role in the team?

The Bottom Line

Inefficiencies are most often caused by a lack of resilience in a system, whether that's you as a whole system, or a process, task, project or whole organisation. Tackling inefficiencies is a good thing for productivity and resilience.

Thereafter productivity gains come from investment in your resilience and in particular your Adaptive Capacity.[23] This covers perspective, energy and realistic pacing. Your Adaptive Capacity gets drained day to day, and must be topped up in order to give you any chance of increasing your success rate.

The Resilience Engine Research Insights

Introduction

Part 2 of this book is dedicated to sharing the highlights of The Resilience Engine's ten years of research insights and implications for human resilience.

The book contains the 'golden nuggets' of the research – those top things that have been proven to make the most difference to our clients. With these golden nuggets, you can create an approach to your own resilience that is simple, practical and transformative. These golden nuggets are what the team and Community of Practice[35] at The Resilience Engine live and breathe in our practice every day. They are most often what our clients need in their first steps into resilience, and will definitely boost your resilience substantially.

For a more detailed investment in you and your team's resilience, we would be delighted to help. The Resilience Engine®,[23] the second research model, is used in our services. Please refer to the Resources section in the book for more details.

Part 2 follows a different chapter structure from Part 1. Each chapter has Overview, Resilience Scene and Bottom Line sections; the other sections vary according to the specific research insight in question.

Chapter 5

The Resilience Dynamic®

'It's like the layers of a golf ball.
Think of all those elastic bands that make up
that golf ball and it's those layers that add to
the strength of that golf ball.'

'(Resilience is a) connector… connectors can be
flexible and supple or they can be really weak and
so, yes, I like that. I think that could maybe
work for people and be a way to explain it.'

Alternative view

I bought my friend an elephant for his room.
He said, 'Thanks.' I said, 'Don't mention it.'

Chapter Overview

This chapter explains the principles behind the Resilience Dynamic®, the first resilience model from The Resilience Engine's research. The model illustrates the nature of resilience, how different states of resilience relate, and the implications for stress, performance and change.

The relationship with wellbeing is weaved throughout this whole chapter, illustrating that the two are entirely synergistic and in fact become the same thing; you cannot have resilience without taking care of yourself and vice versa.

The Resilience Scene

Resilience can seem complicated. There are multiple sources of resilience knowledge and wisdom, and they often seem to be at odds with one another.

Academic research has a strong effect on what we see as the evidence base for what resilience is and how to support it. Whilst this body of knowledge is underpinned by rigorous research methodology, it has focussed in areas where there is a deficit of resilience. Most of the research has been about recovering from adversity:

Resilience research has predominantly focused on individuals who are required – largely through no choice of their own – to react to potentially traumatic events in their lives. Accordingly, theories of resilience have typically been based on clinical populations.[24]

Organisational cultures have a strong effect on views on performance expectations, and where resilience fits in. In some organisational cultures, resilience is a 'no-no' word; it's either about taking more work on without any more capacity, ie work more for less, or where not feeling resilient is an embarrassing admission. Whilst there is more openness now on mental health, closed attitudes still exist. One HR Director within a well-known, successful organisation made this statement in 2017:

people aren't resilient they clearly have psychological issues, and that isn't the stuff for standard organisational training.

Organisations continue to assume that if people need resilience support, they need therapy, and that sits outside of the organisation's remit.

On the other hand, if you are lucky to be working for an organisation where resilience is seen as supporting health and performance, you're onto a winner. Shell Global Health moved their focus away from stress management towards resilience back in 2013. Alastair Fraser, VP of Global Health, called stress management a kind of *'trained helplessness'*, saying it can imply: *'If you don't manage your stress, terrible things will happen.'* This is why Shell shifted its focus from stress to resilience training whereby health is a 'business enabler'.

> *Resilient people are more likely to speak their mind. They are more likely to take principled decisions and are better at tolerating change and pressure. If you want to improve human performance, the key is the person, so how do you give them the tools, techniques and policies to help them deal with a fast-changing world?*
>
> Alistair Fraser, VP Global Health, Shell, speaking at
> Good Day at Work Conference, London, 2013

Popular culture in the west gives us the fundamental idea of persistence: *Nothing ventured, nothing gained,* or *If at first you don't succeed try, try again.* Whilst persistence is part of resilience, if it just means banging your head against a brick wall again and again, it negates wellness.

Two areas that are changing the culture around resilience are the Mindfulness arenas, plus the changing domain of Mental Health where so much is going on to tear down old stigmas of talking about not feeling resilient.

A more transparent way is being forged to tackle mental ill health. Mindfulness practice is a well-researched method that derives from Buddhism; it is now used widely in hospitals and secular settings to reduce stress, depression and anxiety, and improve immune functioning. The essence of mindfulness is to be present to our experience just as it is without judging ourselves.

Mindfulness has a role to play in tackling our mental health crisis in which roughly one in three families include someone who is mentally ill. Up to 10% of the UK adult population will experience symptoms of depression in any given week.

The government's Foresight report developed the concept of mental capital, by which it meant the cognitive and emotional resources that ensured resilience in the face of stress, and the flexibility of mind and learning skills to adapt to a fast-changing employment market and longer working lives. It argued that developing the mental capital of the nation will be 'crucial to our future prosperity and wellbeing'. Qualitative research shows that mindfulness develops exactly these aspects of mental capital, encouraging a curious, responsive and creative engagement to experience.[36]

What if there was something that could join all of these views up in a straightforward way? What if the research on high performance and the research on wellbeing could be put together, so that neither was compromised? That's where The Resilience Engine research comes in.

Definition of Resilience

If you have read the previous chapters, you'll already have an understanding that resilience is your ability to adapt. The measure of your resilience is your capacity for change. Resilience is all about creating options. It's about deliberate investment in that adaptability rather than a singular focus on efficiency as a means of becoming more productive.

Since the capability of adapting is needed in both good times and times of challenge and adversity, resilience is key to success in all situations.

Resilience and wellbeing are interlinked so much that you can't separate one from the other; they are synergistic in all terms. If you invest in your wellbeing, you are investing in your resilience, and vice versa. Resilience encompasses and indeed leverages wellbeing:

o   From The Resilience Engine research, we know that resilience not only includes energy, but that they are directly related; they follow the same ups and downs.

o   Energy encompasses all energy forms: your emotional, physical, mental, and indeed spiritual energy. Energy and wellbeing are effectively the same thing.

o   Strategically resilience and wellbeing become the same thing through this connection to energy. And so throughout the whole book, whenever you read the word 'resilience', please assume it includes wellbeing also.

o   There are component parts of wellbeing where The Resilience Engine's expertise runs out. We are not medical or clinical. We are not experts in nutrition or in the science of physical exercise or sport. We partner with The Healthy Workforce who are experts in these areas, and embed their thinking and models (into our services such as our blended services), so that these components are appropriately enabled in our clients.

The outcome of increased resilience is an increase in wellbeing. Simultaneously you achieve an increase in performance, your success in life. These two drive one of the most wonderful aspects about investment in resilience; your confidence will rise as a result.

The Resilience Dynamic® Model

The Resilience Engine's research shows that there is a contiguous relationship between three principle states of resilience:

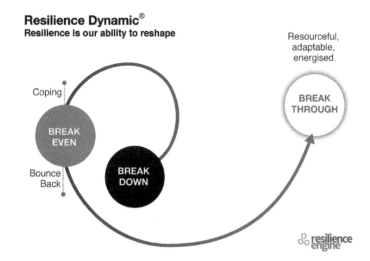

Resilience Dynamic®
Resilience is our ability to reshape

Coping
Bounce Back

BREAK EVEN

BREAK DOWN

Resourceful, adaptable, energised.

BREAK THROUGH

resilience engine

Breakdown where you are not resilient. This coincides completely with what would be classed as a medical Breakdown. It is where you are rendered un-resourceful. There is a catastrophic inability to get hold of the resources inside and where the gap between the resilience demands versus your resilience potential is too great. The gap must be filled initially with the help of others.

Breakeven where you're either Coping, or in Bounceback, or somewhere in between, or indeed oscillating between the two. It's where you go along, churn the usual business, where things are 'ok' or 'fine', but it is difficult to shift to a higher level of performance.

One side of this, Coping, is where things are just manageable. There is no surplus, but things are not broken. The other side, Bounceback, can feel a powerful state, where you punch through challenges. Experiencing the 'ups' of this state can feel like being on top of the world. However, there is a cost attached to Bounceback, which is fatigue.

Your attitude and capacity for change alter substantially depending which side of Breakeven you are on. In Coping, you will resist change; in Bounceback, change is possible. The difference? Your capacity to learn well, which underpins your capacity for change.

Breakthrough is where you have the highest resilience; you embrace change. It's where you are resourceful, adaptable and energised no matter what is going on. You feel at ease in any situation, even if it's new or tricky. You can count on your ability to learn what is needed. Breakthrough is where performance is sustainably high. It involves undoing/redoing solutions all the time. This is part of the Resilient Way and leads to innovation and excellence in leading change.

We call the long line between Breakeven and Breakthrough the 'Whoosh'. This isn't one step, it's a long line of tiny incremental improvements that together shift your resilience towards a level that is both stable and on which you can depend.

Note, movement either up or down through the different resilience levels goes through each of the states in order; you can't skip a step either way. Also note that the model applies to individuals, teams and organisations. It may apply to relationships also but we haven't researched that!

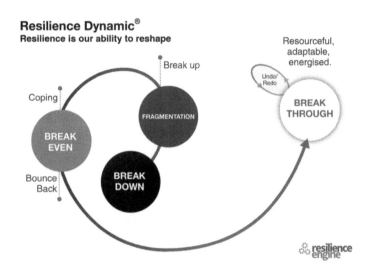

There is one final transition state of resilience that we call **Fragmentation,** in between Coping and Breakdown. It's a pre-Breakdown state, where things begin to break up.

It can often be a hidden state. You don't spot it for yourself very easily. Others around you are more likely to spot clearly that you're 'not coping'. They will notice mood swings, variability in memory, performance and engagement. You will notice this state differently. Sometimes you will feel fine, other times you may feel exhausted or overwhelmed. You may feel 'hard' or 'hardened'; at least very tense. You will suffer from wellness issues such as back problems, your immune system not working and repeated illness. You'll suffer from the negative stress reaction (see Chapter 7 for more on Resilience and Stress).

This is where there is dysfunction within someone, a team or organisation. There are signs of the negative stress reaction really taking over. It is often a stuck state because the person in it cannot get perspective at all, and doesn't have the capacity to stand back. Instead they are entirely buffeted by their circumstances.

Fragmentation is a very difficult and dangerous state for your wellbeing. If someone is in Fragmentation, it is time to act quickly, without hesitation, to enable someone to get back to Coping.

Resilience is in fact safety

As already mentioned in Chapter 2, The Resilience Dynamic® can be read as a contiguous line of a sense of safety.

> *The brain needs to feel safe and protected to guarantee survival before we are likely to be curious, engage in seeking change and new activities that will surely involve some painful moments.*[13]

If you are in Breakdown, you feel unsafe. You are indeed at risk. It is a state of inherent unsafety: someone is not able to keep themselves well and safe mentally or physically and needs help. Breakthrough, on the other hand, is a state of safety.

Someone at Breakthrough resilience trusts wholly that they can keep themselves safe, no matter what is going on. I am not meaning in the face of what is classed as an 'absolute stressor' such as a physical attack; clearly safety will be compromised here. Instead, knowing that you are safe across the normal situations of work and personal life, that's what the highest resilience state is all about.

Those at Breakthrough create and maintain boundaries for themselves. They don't hesitate to call on other resources if need be. It means they are resourceful enough to assess situations and how to navigate them proactively, without bumps or loss. It means they are at ease in their own skin.

When resilience is drained

Here's what happens with low or no resilience:

o   Repeated patterns that don't resolve anything.
o   The continued sense of juggling but being unsure whether you're juggling the right things.
o   Feeling stuck.
o   Loss of perspective and over-reacting to stuff that doesn't merit it.
o   Feeling unwell.
o   Feeling fatigued.
o   Losing confidence.

Without resilience, you experience the negative sides of stress, leading to physical or mental health issues. (See Chapter 7, 'More Resilience = Less Stress', for more information.) This low-resilience state can be normalised if it has lasted a long time and you have almost forgotten what it's like to feel different:

o   Chronic Coping is one state where normalisation has happened.
o   Also even lower, chronic Fragmentation is another.
o   And finally, a third – that difficult and oh-so-fatiguing oscillation between Coping to Fragmentation and back again. This is when you no longer cope, slip back, things get out of control, you galvanise an almighty effort to shift

back again to Coping, clawing at every control mechanism possible, and so it goes until the next slip back. The instability is unpredictable and can feel dangerous. It can be very frustrating which in turn contributes to a resilience drain. Performance and wellness are adversely affected in this high level of oscillation, leading to what we call the Mediocrity Loop.[6]

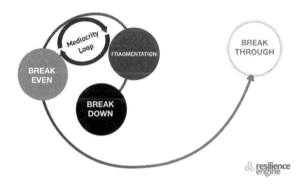

Resilience Dynamic®
Resilience is our ability to reshape

The Mediocrity Loop delivers no change. It delivers getting back to the status quo.

We see this applied often in organisations, where things feel out of control. The organisation is not coping and slips towards Fragmentation. A command and control[37] style of leadership is adopted to ensure that things shift back to a sense of safety, back to Coping. The effort to get there is too much, and resilience slips again, and so the loop continues.

There is the fall-out from the effort of the Mediocrity Loop over and above stuck performance: fatigue and demotivation. Bruised people have witnessed this command and control style overriding their personal voice. And so performance diminishes further.

Key Features of the Resilience Dynamic® Model

Feature 1: The definition is different from the norm

Resilience as your capacity for change is an unusual definition. Most of what is talked about on resilience is about either Coping or about Bounceback. Both of these are elements within resilience, but they do not capture all of what resilience is or indeed can offer. Indeed, both come from a deficit way of thinking.

The deficit of resilience is more researched than higher levels (research titles[38–46] amply demonstrate this), and this dominant discourse has skewed both our understanding and expectations of resilience. The titles of the most recent resilience publications also demonstrate that popular management literature[47–51] explores and supports where there has been difficulty, trauma, a drop in safety, and where you need to be strong. Most of these books are fabulous. They are brilliant in a world that needs to understand and forgive. They are of this time: we all face a lot of difficulty and need to be inspired that we can get through.

Collectively, however, they give a resounding message that resilience is about adversity, challenge and tough stuff, and what you need to do is to get to Bounceback if you can, Coping otherwise. Both Bounceback and Coping are expressed as destinations for resilience development, rather than states that you might pass through.

It is brilliant to cope. It's fantastic to cope when you haven't been doing so. It's brilliant to be in Bounceback after trauma. Oh my goodness, isn't that just amazing, that you can experience joy and wonder and curiosity again? And it's not the whole story. Resilience development doesn't need to end at Coping or Bounceback. There are other higher states of resilience that are attainable for everyone. These are where you feel at ease, where many of the bumps of life are smoothed out before they arise, where trauma isn't the thing, and instead it's about living more fully.

Feature 2: Resilience is dynamic

One of the keys to understanding the nature of resilience is that it goes up and down, and that this is completely normal:

○ It goes up and down according to health.

○ It goes up when you get a lovely hug from your kids in the morning. Or better still, you all have a habit of hugging one another in the morning every day. Each morning it's like rolling up at the resilience petrol station.

○ It goes up and down according to how much is left in the 'reservoir' of your resilience that you use each day. If you've been running yourself down across many months and hit a challenge, it will seem huge in comparison to its real size. Your resilience will be more drained as a result: you'll over-egg the emotions needed to get through it, over-egg the solution needed, and spend more energy on it than it merits. Thus you'll contribute to a resilience drain, the opposite of what you need.

○ It goes up when you successfully turn the corner after a long-term challenge, when you have held onto hope that something will change for the better, kept open to the possibilities and opportunities to make that a reality, managed those opportunities as best as you can. You can feel proud that you got through.

Accept that your resilience will go up and down, it's that simple. It might mean getting over yourself, or at least keeping your ego in check.

For those with the highest resilience, they accept this. They don't fight it. If there's a serious challenge, they remove other non-essential tasks, they focus on resourcing themselves. They account for the challenge proactively and quickly. And they expect of themselves that their performance in whatever domain will be more variable. No big deal.

Those with the highest resilience allow themselves the best chance at getting through any challenge, so they can recover quickly to return to feeling more at ease. Their acceptance allows them to navigate challenges in the easiest way possible.

The key to operating like this is awareness. You've got to get hold of the data associated with your resilience, not be shy of it, look at it straight, see the truth of what is going on, and act on it.

Feature 3: Being in more than one state

This is also normal. You might be thriving at work, but Coping at home. Or the other way around.

Your overall resilience is a combination of all of your resilience states. Thus if you thrive in work at what might be considered high up on the Whoosh, but have a relationship difficulty with your partner at home where you are Coping, you will end up somewhere like Bounceback as your average. That means in reality you will sometimes thrive, sometimes cope, and often be feeling that up and down curve, and so be tired a lot of the time. That is a resilience drain in itself.

For you to be at one state, you have to have consistent resilience in all the areas of your life.

For you to be at the highest level of resilience, at Breakthrough, your resilience needs to be context-free. That means that you've learnt the conditions for you to feel safe in your own skin. It is the experience of The Resilience Engine that senior leaders often imagine they have this highest level, but in truth, their resilience is often lower, somewhere on the Whoosh. They are very comfortable where they are but rarely go into zones where they are really uncomfortable. That lack of stretch or lack of new learning means they end up stuck: they're successfully on the Whoosh whilst things remain the same, but may drop to Coping when there is an unexpected challenge or change of context. That drop can be a real shock.

The work of the Whoosh towards Breakthrough is stepping into discomfort somewhere in your life. I don't mean tired, or overworked, or just maxed out. I mean uncomfortable and having to learn.

Feature 4: Gender differences

Please read this section knowing that it is best-intentioned. The Resilience Engine research uncovered a difference in the resilience data regarding gender difference. We do not necessarily like the answer, but it is strongly evidenced.

It is an inescapable output of the first stage of The Resilience Engine research that women rate their own resilience 20% lower than men do. As a woman, I was annoyed when I saw this. Then I had this marvellous thought, was it more our perceptions of ourselves than the actual way resilience played out in our behaviour and our results; did we in fact have an equal or even higher resilience level? I wondered if it might be the phenomenon whereby women rate themselves lower than men, but it isn't actually true. This phenomenon is present in many places and shows that women are more likely to experience 'Imposter Syndrome' than men.[38,52–56]

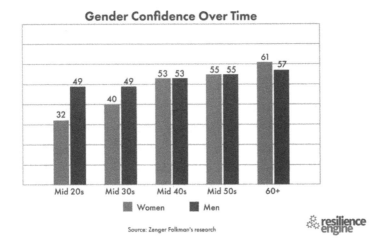

Gender Confidence Over Time

Source: Zenger Folkman's research

Source: Based on data from Forbes.com article *'The Confidence Gap in Men and Women: Why It Matters and How to Overcome It'* by Jack Zenger.

I decided to be curious, open and see what would come up in the validation process of the research findings. I spent quite a few years looking for a different answer in the resilience stories of our clients. I got back the same overarching data with an important qualification:

Women's resilience is lower than men's resilience probably to the tune of 20% but only at the higher levels of resilience. Further towards Breakeven, resilience kicks in more strongly in women than in men.

Women are brilliant at Coping, especially long-term Coping. Women can sustain this level of just managing for a long time, quite accepting that this is the way it is. When faced with something really tough, women shift into Coping mode, and strongly commit to not cracking. *'I'll survive'* or *'I'll get through this'* is the motto. The skills for long-term Coping are multiple. Included is women's approach to life: a more collaborative way than what has been shown as a more agentic style amongst men:

> *Men are associated with 'agentic' behavior, meaning that they tend to be proactive, assertive, dominant, and in control of situations. By contrast, women are associated with 'communal values', such as friendliness, support, and a warm and caring attitude. When we look at these two sets of traits, it becomes clear that the agentic approach is the one we associate with leadership.*
>
> Professor Ginka Toekel, IMD
> Business School, Switzerland

Thus women reach out to friends, family, colleagues to help them to cope with the situation.

However, men give themselves more opportunity for higher resilience than women do. One of the key characteristics of women's resilience, or what holds their resilience back, is a special barrier all to themselves. Give a clap for the phenomenon of superwoman!

The Superwoman Syndrome:

Women rate their resilience 20% lower than men do (and it's true)!

- GOALS
  Don't stick to meaningful goals!
- REFRESH
  Don't refresh themselves.
- PACING
  Poor pacing.
- IMPORTANCE
  Incomplete self acceptance - as consider themselves less important.

ACCEPTANCE
Incomplete self acceptance - Need to be liked.

FIXER
Fixer of all problems!

03

02

01

EXPECTATION
Unrealistic expectation of capacity

Whilst it might seem fantastic to model ourselves on superwoman, we are not just holding back our resilience but we are actually draining it:

o   Women have an unrealistic view of their own capacity. This gives rise to a drain in energy, which in turn reduces their flexibility.

At the heart of this, women don't refresh themselves as well as men. We put ourselves last. Our nurture kicks in: we want to make sure everyone else is ok, then we think of ourselves. Men will, more often than women, refresh themselves as a norm.

o Women don't accept themselves as well as men do.

   Self-acceptance or the lack of it is key here. It is often labelled as an issue of female confidence but we see it more simply than that: women have more difficulty in accepting themselves than men. See more in Chapter 3 on confidence.

o Women take on the responsibility of ensuring everyone else feels ok. In doing so they seek to fix everything. Whether it's theirs to fix, or whether it's fixable, or whether other people want them to, women want to fix things. This in turn destroys their energy; they can be 'off purpose' doing stuff that others want them to do, and they also detract from accepting situations for what they are. These are all destroyers of resilience.

The resilience gender difference might be in the process of changing. The data from The Resilience Engine is skewed towards leaders and managers, probably mostly of ages 35 and upwards. Could it be that those of us who are middle aged and whose mothers didn't work have learnt the value of acting as superwomen? Perhaps. The Resilience Engine has the impression that the current data we have tells us more about our past than it does about our future. We have hope!

91

Implications of the Resilience Dynamic® Model

Implication 1: Resilience and stress

🔍 Review

o   Where do you think the highest negative stress is experienced in The Resilience Dynamic®?

o   When have you experienced high stress in your work or personal life? What resilience level did you have at the time?

o   Have you experienced the difference between short-term negative stress and long-term negative stress? What are the implications for yourself in each of these situations?

Breakdown is a state where the lack of resilience is evident. If the person gets help, normally the main stressors are removed instantly and the stress reaction reduces. Removing the main stressors helps enormously; it releases the pressure. The person can start to move some basic recovery mechanisms in place, like sleep, gentle movement, being with others that care, eating well; the basics.

Negative stress can continue to exist in Breakdown for quite some while. On top of any physical impact, which may be substantial, there is the need to understand the sources of the Breakdown, work through these, and importantly, forgive – both yourself and others. Not forgiving, holding up some kind of bar to how you/they should have been, how you/they should have reacted, how you/they should have managed, leads to negative stress. Letting this bar go, accepting that your resilience was rock bottom and you/they couldn't be resourceful, is the pathway to forgiveness. You may need to forgive yourself just as much as forgiving others. That in turn releases more resilience potential.

Fragmentation is the resilience level most dominated on an ongoing basis by negative stress. Someone is really held hostage to the negative stress reaction: that cortisol/adrenalin hijack that takes over, that leads to unwellness and poor mental functioning.

Coping is also stress-oriented. This is not as strong as within Fragmentation. If you're Coping, you are managing the negative stress. Just! But nevertheless you are managing. Maybe sometimes it's tough to do so, but you're keeping it together as long as nothing else pushes you over the edge.

Then there is the last area – the oscillation between Coping and Fragmentation, if you're caught in the Mediocrity Loop. What a pain that back and forth, it's the movement, it's the continual slipping back that really is resilience draining, on top of a situation where you have no excess capacity in the first place.

The higher states of resilience have a completely different relation to stress. At Bounceback, stressors still exist of course, but there can be an odd mix depending on where you are in the up and down curve:

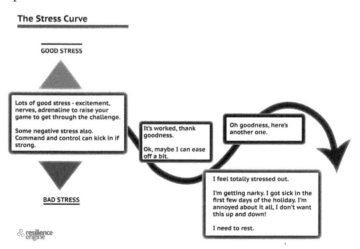

The Stress Curve

GOOD STRESS

Lots of good stress - excitement, nerves, adrenaline to raise your game to get through the challenge.

Some negative stress also. Command and control can kick in if strong.

It's worked, thank goodness.

Ok, maybe I can ease off a bit.

Oh goodness, here's another one.

BAD STRESS

I feel totally stressed out.

I'm getting narky. I got sick in the first few days of the holiday. I'm annoyed about it all, I don't want this up and down!

I need to rest.

resilience engine

At Bounceback you feel negative stress when you are in one of the 'downs', where energy is very low. This is short-lived, however, since you will rise again at the next challenge. However, if there are multiple challenges at the same time, you may end up in Coping mode, and this induces longer term negative stress.

In Breakthrough, you don't experience negative stress. You just don't. You have the stressors of course, but you don't experience a hijack of stress. You instead experience excitement. Most likely of all, you are experiencing a pretty stable life as the dark line below shows:

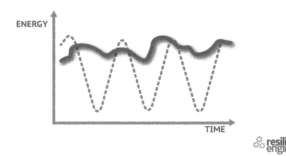

For further information on Resilience and Stress, see Chapter 7.

Implication 2: Resilience and change

🔍 Review

Where is change possible on The Resilience Dynamic®? Which resilience states can embrace change?

When have you experienced a real drive for change in your work or personal life? What resilience level did you have at the time?

Consider your team:

o   When can the team take on change? What is the collective resilience of the team at that point?

o   When can the team not manage change well? What is the collective resilience of the team at that point?

o   Notice the difference.

⇨ Change

How can you foster higher resilience levels in yourself so that you find change easy?

How can you foster the resilience of your team to be able to take on change more easily?

Change is possible in The Resilience Dynamic® at the following levels:

o   At Breakthrough, where change is the norm.

o   Along the Whoosh, most of the time. If high on the Whoosh, practically all the time, but if lower – say, just along a bit from Bounceback – the capacity for change varies.

o   At Bounceback in the 'up' bits, and indeed in the 'down' bits as long as you're not totally knackered and slipped back to Coping and have destroyed your capacity for learning.

At Bounceback, however, some changes may never happen. If you have a deep resistance to one or two things, there will be no change.

o   At Coping there is no real change. Small changes are possible, the kind of stuff that is within your comfort zone already such as processes at work, tidying your desk, going to bed a bit earlier, or getting a handle on your to-do list. But significant change isn't possible here. Even if you wanted to change, you just don't have capacity.

🔍 Review

Think about all of that in your leadership position. How many of your staff are at the Coping level of resilience? What change are you expecting them to embrace?

These staff cannot adopt any significant change until their resilience levels are higher. That means the work of your leadership needs to foster the conditions for resilience such as energy, role clarity, perspective, strict prioritisation and collaboration. For further information on Resilience and Change, see Chapter 8.

Implication 3: Resilience and control

If you've read Chapter 2, you know that it's just a myth that for resilience you need control. Instead you need to take both the responsibility and, as appropriate, the accountability for your actions, plus control when necessary. Control really isn't the thing to get your knickers in a twist about at all. Taking responsibility, that's the core of it all.

🔍 Review

This exercise can be done together with your team.

Consider for your team where the drive for control shows up most.

At Breakdown, you cannot take control because you're at risk. You are normally helped by those who do take control over some aspects of your health and wellbeing, like your doctor.

At Fragmentation, you seek to get back to Coping because things are way out of control. If you can, you grab any means to get back in control. In deep Fragmentation, however, you've probably shifted quite a bit away from being resourceful enough to take back control. You are buffeted about. And if you can't gain some control back, you need immediate help, because you are shifting towards Breakdown.

In Coping, you keep control of everything you can because it's the way to manage. By controlling, you keep your head above water.

In Bounceback, you may or may not seek control. It depends on whether your start point is higher or lower:

From Coping

You probably hold onto control in a big way because that's what you have learnt helps you to cope better.

Or

From the Whoosh

You'll be more laid back about control. On the Whoosh and higher, you get into holding responsibility and accountability, and let go more and more of control.

For further information on Resilience and Control, see Chapter 2.

What Resilience Is Not!

You will have read in Chapters 1–4 how to loosen the grip of certain myths of resilience that may have taken hold of you! Here they are again just as a quick recap:

o   From Myth 1: Resilience is **not** being tough.
    Toughness in the long term leads to brittleness, the opposite of adaptability.

    The Resilient Way is all about creating options.

o   From Myth 2: Resilience is **not** becoming a control freak.
    The relationship between resilience and control is not direct; you do not need one for the other.

    The Resilient Way is to choose how and whether to exercise control. Those with the highest resilience take responsibility first and foremost, accountability also where appropriate. And they control what they need to, but let go of control of everything else. And feel fine about that!

o   From Myth 3: Confidence is **not** needed to become resilient. The relationship between resilience and confidence is not one-way, but in fact two-way.

    The Resilient Way means investing in learning in order to increase self-efficacy in relation to things you do. It also means drawing on and investing in secure bases, those things in life that give you a sense of security and inspiration. This process is two-way.

o   From Myth 4: Driving efficiency delivers the highest productivity.

There is an incessant pressure to be more efficient. But efficiency will only get you so far; thereafter, resilience is needed.

The Resilient Way includes tackling obvious inefficiencies. Thereafter investment needs to be made in your Adaptive Capacity, the fuel of your resilience that gets used up day to day. By doing this you can double your capacity and release your creativity, and these together deliver a transformative level of performance or productivity.

The Resilient Way

Becoming aware of your own reactions and responses is your first step towards your own understanding of resilience. This is all about learning to read the resilience data from your own resilience and that of your team. The data gives you the first step in understanding how to manage and extend your resilience. As Ruby Wax says in her book *Sane New World: Taming the Mind*[57]: *'It's not giving yourself a hard time for going nuts – because we usually get stressed about stress.'*

The next step is to loosen the grip of your barriers to resilience. The conditions that drain or hold back your resilience are as important as how to enable a resilience extension. Thereafter it's about setting up the conditions for your resilience to flourish. Your own resilience depends on whether you manage the day-to-day conditions to help you thrive. You may notice that if you haven't rested you're more prone to heightened emotional reactions. If you haven't had time with friends, you may notice that you become locked into a particular perspective, maybe serious or focussed or even 'heavy'. If you haven't connected with what's important to you, you can feel frustrated and demotivated.

Each person's set of resilience conditions is personal. Taken from the application of The Resilience Engine® model and methods of working with thousands of people, we offer the Top Enablers of resilience. Part 3 of the book explores these in depth.

Applying the Resilient Way

The Resilience River

© The Resilience Engine 2019

The idea of checking into the levels of your resilience on the Resilience Dynamic® can be done simply using this metaphor:

 Review

Consider resilience is like a river.
It comes from a deep reservoir.

When the river flows, it flows beautifully! When the river is high, the water whooshes over the rocks, it's not taken off course, and the rocks need to be respected but are not dominant. Things flow.

When the river is low, it's the opposite. Rocks are felt much more, they hurt when you bang into them; even the small ones. Things are way out of perspective. What is actually a small rock or even a pebble can seem huge, if the river level is low. The river can be split or indeed pushed off course. There is tremendous effort in getting a good flow, of moving towards where the river needs to go.

Knowing where your own resilience is at any one moment helps you understand the capacity you have for what you have to do. It defines your performance. It defines your ability to drive towards a set of goals, or whether you can be taken off course. It defines the pace you can operate at. It defines whether you feel good or not good.

Your Resilience River underpins all your sustainable success in life.

✏ Change

Using the Resilience River day to day
There are two ways of using the Resilience River:

1. As a barometer for the day/week ahead.

    This supports what leadership and management literature, plus those in sports, call 'state management'.[24,107] Check in. What is the level of your Resilience River today? What will the implications be?

If the river is low-ish, you are likely to bang hard into some big rocks, whilst perhaps able to whoosh over some of the rubbishy pebbles that are sitting on the river bed. If that's the case, what can you do to allow yourself the best chance during this day:

> What can you say 'no' to?
>
> What could you delay so that you don't have to face it today?
>
> How can you get more energy for when you do have to navigate around the big rocks?

If the river is choppy, you are likely to feel unstable.

> What can you do to feel more stable today?
>
> How can you allow yourself to 'be present' more?
>
> Who can help?

If the river is high, how can you really maximise this day?

> What are the opportunities that are afforded by this level of resilience?
>
> Do you want to reconfigure your day to take advantage of these?

2. As a means to discover what you want to change in your life.

Check in to your river across a period of time – say the past three to six months, or the past year.

What has the level of your Resilience River been like? How has it been? The proxy for doing this in detail is to check your Energy Mapping (see Chapter 9). Using the Resilience River analogy might allow you to do this in your head, and a bit more simply.

If it's been really low, what is going on?

If those rocks are still there, and you really are fed up with them now, how can you shift them?

Your Resilience River can give you indications for what you need to learn, in order to shift the whole thing to a great flow.

Stories of Resilience

Extract from resilience diary of client

I am feeling really fatigued. A long-term set of issues have been running in my work life for a long time now, and whilst I as the leader am the carrier of the 'light', the one that is supposed to absorb anxiety, the one that carries the vision, I am losing my trust in that vision, and can often feel overwhelming.

I have a task to do today that is really important, and normally motivating. I have assigned this one day to it. What a gift of time! It will not be available to me after today so I need to do it.

But I start the day with checking in on the big issue, and that leaves me in a low state, with little energy and little motivation. I have to drive to where I am going. I talk to myself as I drive – 'not sure how on earth this is going to work'; ' I wonder if I should leave'; ' I've been over-ambitious'; ' I am not sure how to face the troops'. And so it goes.

It's a sunny day. It's incredibly beautiful. I am going to a beautiful location for this task, it's a good place for me. And I carry in the task all the wishes that I would ever have for the business, but also for what it means to my family and friends, what they wish for me. Their wishes and love are with me. I feel them with me.

I arrive at my destination. I don't dive into the task immediately. I give myself the opportunity to breathe, to have a bit of a walk outside, to feel all this positive energy. I move, I walk with purpose, stretching my body out, so it too starts to feel awakened. I am beginning to unlock something inside myself. I am proud of myself for turning my state around, and knowing that I can do this big, important task today. I am ready.

I feel oh-so-much-better! And so I do well in that task for the day, holding onto all the resilience-supporting assets that are part of me. And in doing well at that task too, I know it will positively influence things towards resolution.

This is a resilient response to a long-term resilience drain. I didn't expect myself to just switch. I gave myself every opportunity to do the important big task really well. My resilience went up, and it will no doubt go down again. But for this one day, I did a good job, and will sleep well.

The Resilience Lens

This person is feeling under pressure and is really tired from it. They are at best in Bounceback, but may be heading for Coping because of how tired they are. They have a wonderfully motivating thing to do in this day, and are aware it's really special to get a day out. This is a sign of awareness, so they are already skilled in this.

They are weighed down by a big issue, which renders them near Coping. However, they can resource themselves to take and leverage this one day for themselves. They do this well. They do not take it for granted and instead give themselves time and space.

☉ The Resilience Lens

Which resilience levels did this person pass through?

How do you account for changes in your resilience levels?

How do you resource yourself when your resilience is lower than you need it to be?

The Bottom Line

This chapter has outlined the definition of resilience and implications for stress, change and performance through the lens of The Resilience Dynamic®. This single model provides a map of how all resilience states connect to one another. It also highlights some of the key insights on resilience. There are very simple and profound implications:

o The outcomes of resilience are wellbeing and performance; neither is compromised.
o Resilience is dynamic, and will shift up and down due to context.
o Very low levels of resilience are not always spotted by the person; others need to help.
o Coping and below is where the negative stress reaction will dominate. See more in Chapter 7 for how stress works.

o   Those with the highest levels of resilience do not suffer from the negative stress reaction, although they will experience the same kinds of stressors as anyone else.

The Resilience Engine experience shows that understanding the nature of resilience provides a real gateway to clarity and practical action towards increasing it.

The Different Levels of Resilience: Where Are You?

*'The point of inflection towards resilience is
where the personal cost is minimal'*

'I think my resilience is going down. I take less risks.'

Alternative views

Never trust atoms. They make up everything.

Chapter Overview

This chapter sets out to help you get really clear about your own resilience levels. If you're thinking of your team, colleagues or indeed family and friends as you read the book, this will help you be clear about their resilience levels too.

Start with your own resilience self-evaluation. This is done as a straight-off-the-bat exercise on the basis of what you know so far. (You are welcome to use a more comprehensive self-evaluation tool for free. Our Resilience Check-in© can be found on our home page: www.resilienceengine.com.)

Next, read the detail behind each main resilience level so that you can spot the associated behaviours. The usual tools and stories are included at the end of the chapter.

The Resilience Scene

Most people understand the Resilience Dynamic® model quickly. They can gauge their own resilience level without too much cognitive processing. Even if they are in more than one place at the same time because of different contexts, it's pretty straightforward.

Then their brain kicks in and they want to be sure. Until they're really sure, they won't act. This cognitive interrupt lets them off the hook in terms of taking responsibility. Until they know more, they won't take responsibility for their own resilience. So nothing will change. To alter this we name the need to 'Bypass the Cognitive Faff' in our 'Ten Principles of Enabling The Resilient Organisation' (sign up via the website: www.resilienceengine.com to our publications to receive a copy).

The first real challenge of enabling your own resilience is to be truthful with yourself. It could be convenient in the short term to remain in some kind of denial. Dr Gleb Tsipursky,[58] a behavioural scientist of Ohio State University who researches denialism, talks about an interesting dynamic that happens:

> Someone is in denial. They may exhibit the Ostrich effect.[59,60] They refute the facts, or indeed, may spread mistruths. Your instinct is to confront them with the facts of the situation. You get the *'backfire effect'*:

> *Research on a phenomenon called the backfire effect shows we tend to dig in our heels when we are presented with facts that cause us to feel bad about our identity, self-worth, worldview or group belonging... In some cases, presenting the facts actually backfires, causing people to develop a stronger attachment to incorrect beliefs. Moreover, we*

express anger at the person bringing us the message, a phenomenon researchers term 'shoot the messenger.'

What Tsipursky talks about is that it's not the facts that are the issue. To change the situation or outcome, you need to confront the emotions that lie behind facing the facts. However, there are multiple possible interference effects.

There is confirmation bias.[61–64]

Imagine that you believe that you are a person that always gets through challenges, no matter what. It's part of who you are: you just keep persisting, you punch through. Your workplace loves you, you are the person to go to when there are challenges, people can count on you! It has become part of how you see yourself, and what you're proud of.

Then one day the demands placed upon you are too great. For example, the workload has become unbearable because you're having to implement a massive structural change. How to do it all?

The resilience demand is now higher than your resilience potential. You struggle. You see the multiple challenges involved. You battle each one. But you are becoming more and more fatigued, and you are beginning to lose perspective. It flares up even at home. The issue affects you at home and that leakage makes you feel more unsettled, less secure, less able to cope. You start to doubt yourself, your performance is dropping and you don't know what to do. You are stuck and you feel a bit helpless.

Your own confirmation bias tells you that you always get through challenges. To accept that you can't get through a challenge destroys that same identity. It hurts to accept it. But in that inflexible response to the reality of the situation, you deny a truth. Not accepting the situation truthfully means you don't look for other solutions and options early. You end up in a stuck situation of not managing to stem a significant resilience drain. That leads to not coping, and that can lead into unwellness.

It's not good.

Or.

There is the sunk cost fallacy.[65–68]

There is the denial that a past decision was not good, and instead, you keep with the same solution, denying that it's not working. Tsipursky[58] has a good example':

In another example at a company where I consulted, a manager refused to acknowledge that a person hired directly by her was a bad fit, despite everyone else in the department telling me that the employee was holding back the team. The manager's behavior likely resulted from what scholars term the sunk cost fallacy, a tendency to double down on past decisions even when an objective assessment shows the decision to be problematic.

It's not good.

Or.

You genuinely haven't experienced another way.

Imagine you are a high performer. That means working long hours, working weekends, taking on more projects, saying yes to the tough stuff, being flexible but also tough.

How did all of those ideas become your norm? Perhaps from your upbringing which has become reinforced in your organisation and maybe even by friends. You may not have experienced another way of being. You may consider that this is the only way: long hours are needed. Even if others tell you it's not, even if you read all the books in the world that tell you a different way to handle things, you can't see it, you can't understand it, it's not real, it's the stuff of fairy tales.

Without another perspective, how could you consider anything different? Being resilient means seeking other perspectives all the time. In the Resilient Way there is always another way.

All of these factors, the confirmation bias, the sunk cost fallacy, and just the sheer lack of experience, end up with a denial about the facts of the situation, and all are used to avoid truth. The experience of truth-facing can be negative because it can rock identity, even if identity is part false.

The fact that an identity is not flexible enough to take account of changing circumstances or indeed mistakes is in itself resilience data. When you hold onto an identity where there is no room for change on a particular topic or you can't accept that you will make mistakes, where will it lead you? To stuckness. And to an inevitable resilience drain.

Facing the truth of your resilience is your first act of investing in your performance and wellbeing. By understanding and accepting your current resilience potential versus the resilience demand upon you, you can really start to generate options early, which helps you thrive more.

Living in a Resilient Way builds on this truth. Being truthful gives you a real baseline for what to expect in any situation. That can feel:

o like relief and therefore lighter. That already contributes to your resilience.
o like a wake-up call, and therefore you know you need help to change your situation. That contributes to your resilience.
o really humbling, you can feel really grateful. That positive, grateful attitude continues to sustain your resilience.

Evaluating Your Own Resilience

The right state of mind for truth

🔍 **Review**

What is your mind like right now? Take a moment to think about it.

This really is about you and getting quality space and time to reflect on yourself and your resilience.

o You may want to consider where you do this reflection. Are you in the best environment for you to connect with yourself and think? If not, where is?

o You may want to consider when you do this reflection. Is this the right time to think about this kind of thing? Are you jamming reading this in between stuff? Do you have space for it?

Maybe at the beginning or end of the day might be better to consider your resilience, so you can take your thoughts that come up, and enjoy musing or considering them. Enjoy slowing down. Let your thoughts about your own resilience just come to you. If you don't want to, there is no need to attach much meaning at all, just let them wash over you.

The key to getting the most out of this chapter, and indeed this book, is to give yourself some slow-down space.

Self-evaluation

You've probably got the hang of The Resilience Dynamic® model already.

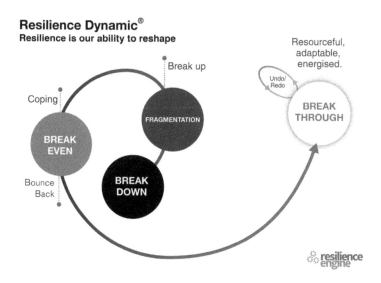

Resilience Dynamic®
Resilience is our ability to reshape

✍ Write down

Where are you on The Resilience Dynamic®?

Notice immediately where you think you are on The Resilience Dynamic®.

If you haven't had the chance to really go into the Resilience Dynamic® yet, do give yourself a chance by reading Chapter 5. Choose to evaluate your resilience against a time frame that is relevant for you. It could be today, this week. Or it could be over a period of 2–3 months. Or it could be more generally, this half of the year for example.

Write where you think you are.

If you're not sure, or if you could be in several states at the same time depending on the context, or if you're a bit nervous of really saying where you think you are, take your time.

You are welcome to use a more comprehensive self-evaluation tool for free. Our Resilience Check-in© can be found on our home page: www.resilienceengine.com.

🔍 Review

How do you feel about that state/those states of resilience for yourself?

o   Satisfied?
o   Concerned?
o   Feeling a bit more confident?
o   Overwhelmed?
o   Worried?
o   Intrigued?
o   Frustrated?
o   Bored?

Your resilience story will depend on how much you take responsibility for it. You can make a step towards that by taking responsibility for what you've noticed so far.

Review

Further questions you may have:

Are you in one state or more than one? What does that mean?

Are you shifting between states often? Within the same week? Within the same day?

Do you know what it's like at a higher level of resilience? Have you been there before?

Change

If you find your resilience is shifting, what do you need to stabilise it at the higher level? Stabilising your resilience is often the initial goal. That can give you a real sense of steadiness, a firm platform to build on.

If you want to invest in a higher resilience, what level might you realistically get to in the next month?

The Resilience States in More Detail

You have now read the theory of resilience via The Resilience Dynamic®. You are starting to understand the implications for yourself and your team. You may still doubt your own judgement, especially about your team. Indeed making assumptions about the resilience levels of each of your team members can lead to interference or to misjudgements.

To check your assessment out more specifically, use the following tables that explain each resilience level in detail.

Breakthrough resilience

Breakthrough is the highest level of resilience possible. When you are at Breakthrough resilience, you are resourceful, adaptable and energised, no matter what is going on. Your resources are not hijacked by anything, you maintain perspective and options, and have surplus energy. You can see joy, even when things are tough.

Stress isn't really felt negatively at all here; instead you have an enormous capacity for what you do.

This is when you are fully at ease making changes. It's a strategic capability in business and organisations. It's a strategic capability in your personal life; to thrive no matter what life throws up.

If you enter into completely new contexts that are challenging, you accept that you need to re-learn how to get to Breakthrough. During this time, there may be a slip back down the Whoosh. Knowing yourself and what has brought you to Breakthrough before is immensely helpful in enabling you to learn fast about how to achieve it in a new context. You are confident that you can learn again, and this accelerates the rise of your resilience.

Breakthrough is the resilience level where deficit doesn't play a part. It is also the point in the Resilience Dynamic® which ensures a sustainable high performance.

Breakthrough: How do you know?

Here's the fast-track.

Observable Behaviour	Open and curious, good learner
	Says 'no' often
	Great delegator
	Prepared to change – but at the same time decisive, clear and driven
	Seems to take it all in their stride

	Takes care of themselves – sleep, physical exercise, time out, fresh air, decent nutrition
	Laughs often
	Lives life to the full
Internal Talk	I am so fortunate
	What is coming down the line that I need to consider?
	Does this matter?
	This is unexpectedly difficult. What do I need to account for whilst dealing with this?
	Do I have enough resources for this right now?
	What can help in this situation? Who can help me?
	That's done, now I can go and… switch off/be with the family/read the paper… yay!
What You Feel	Lucky
	Humble
	Empowered
	Energetic
	Steady in life
	Healthy
	Generous
	Calm
Relationship with Stress	Life is good. It might be busy, but it's all good
Relationship with Change	Bring it on, as long as it's within my/our capacity
Relationship with Control	Most of the time it's unnecessary to Control much, it doesn't get you very far

On the Whoosh

Once you are on the road to higher resilience, you feel really different. Stress doesn't really figure here in the same way. Instead of stress, you absorb pressure. That means your tipping point for stress is pretty far away.

Going round the Whoosh feels great. It's freeing. You have enough capacity for doing many more of the things you want to do. You have sorted a lot of your relationships out. You perform well. And you are living in a more balanced and integrated way.

However, you may not be like this in all domains. It's possible, for example, that you may have been in a leadership position for several years within the same organisation. Day to day, you operate within this comfort zone where your resilience is high and not really under any new demand. The Resilience Engine works with many managers and leaders, who experience shock when there is a sudden drop in their resilience due to a new kind of resilience demand. Whilst someone can think their resilience is at Breakthrough level, when faced with something very challenging – it could be redundancy, say, or a health issue, or a great loss – they can become lost; normally that person's resilience level has been in the middle of the Whoosh, but not higher.

Being on the Whoosh can also feel unstable. You can be enticed by the release of capacity that you find yourself with into taking more on. Then you will experience a slip back. You venture back up the Whoosh, but it may happen several times. Many leaders and managers find the Whoosh both a great and a frustrating state!

As you journey along the Whoosh towards higher resilience, you need to learn to let go of things and that can feel uncomfortable. At the same time, once through this stage, you will feel more and more at ease, and that feels light, freeing and easy. Getting to stability at the higher levels takes work; the Whoosh is one long line symbolically to indicate this work: it takes time and attention to achieve Breakthrough.

On the Whoosh: How do you know?

Here's the fast track.

Observable Behaviour	Open and curious, good learner on most things. May reject the need to learn in one or two areas (blind spots)
	When in comfort zone (which in itself incorporates an ability to be uncomfortable), performs really well. Has one or two domains which are off-limits
	Laughs a lot. But really doesn't laugh if feels negatively exposed in any way
	Lives life to the full, within their defined, comfortable areas
	Likely to take care of themselves mostly, although may be prone to sacrificing some of wellbeing for work/other matters
	Says 'no' often
	Great delegator
	Prepared to change – but at the same time decisive, clear and driven.
Internal Talk	Life is great
	I love this, I love being at my best and enabling others to be there too
	When in comfort zone – How does this matter? What's coming down the line?
	What's the best choice – eg sacrifice family time in the short term for this?

	What can help in this situation? Who can help me? Except in a couple of key areas where the response will be – 'no thanks, I don't need your help on that one'
What You Feel	Lucky and deserved
	Powerful and empowered
	Satisfied
	Pretty healthy – what you might expect for this level of job/pressure/life
	Mostly generous except when significantly diverted away from purpose
Relationship with Stress	Life is good. Busy of course!
Relationship with Change	I am the responsible one, of course, bring it to me
Relationship with Control	You can't control that much in the end. I always have liked control, but I have learnt how to get that through others

Bounceback

Bounceback is recovery from setback or trauma.

When you're in Bounceback, you have already figured that you can recover from setbacks. You experience stress and you have learnt how to handle it pretty well. You may persist but experience fatigue.

You are likely to know yourself quite well in order to reach and remain at Bounceback. This knowledge will form part of the strategy for maintaining Bounceback. For example, if you know that you can 'lose the plot' sometimes and get angry, especially when you're tired, you'll be figuring out ways to increase your energies. That might mean pacing your work better, delegating more, switching off at weekends. You'll do these things because you **know them to work**. And that means your ability to absorb pressure will be higher, and that means your tipping point into stress will be further away than for others.

The difficulty with Bounceback is that if there are too many setbacks close together, you lose the energy to deal with them successfully and so you slip back to Coping. You may exhibit tension, rigidity. You may start to dominate certain conversations. In the workplace, often those in Bounceback under a lot of pressure will not want to drop their performance, and instead start to defend their performance by behaving more in command and control[37] mode.

Bounceback is inherently unstable because of the ups and downs involved. The diagram below shows a typical energy graph of someone in Bounceback; highs of energy are needed to get through challenges, followed by the aftermath of fatigue.

The Instability Of Bounceback

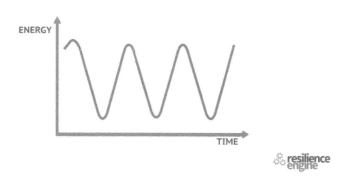

Being in Bounceback can also be fragile; you can slip back to Coping if you don't shift towards a more stable state.

Bounceback: How do you know?

Here's the fast track.

Observable Behaviour	Says 'yes' to many things
	Says 'I can' to many things
	Enjoys a challenge
	Persistent
	Looks for solutions
	Wants to be noticed, wants praise
	Can get prickly or tired in the middle of challenge
Internal Talk	I really want them to see I can do a good job. I have to, otherwise they won't respect me
	It's part of climbing the ladder
	Go, go, go! Keep going!
	It's ok to do longer hours, it'll be just for a while
	If I can just get through this, I'll then get the space to think and see what the real priority is
What You Feel	Mix of excitement and nervousness
	Loving the high
	Loving the sense of achievement
	Loving that others need you
	Loving the juggle, it's hard and interesting and challenging
	Fatigue can set in if challenge lasts a long time
	Fatigue, annoyance and irritation if juggling too many balls
	Sometimes weary to be asked again – why is it always me that gets asked?

Relationship with Stress	Knows a lot about it, can manage it often, but still keeps getting caught by it
Relationship with Change	Loves it. But doesn't always have space or capacity for it, and sometimes does not have capacity for the learning necessary to enact the change
Relationship with Control	Seeks it in the down parts of the up and down curve

In the middle of Breakeven

There are three ways into this state of being right in the middle of Breakeven:

Case 1: You have been there for ages, you're a bit stuck.
Case 2: You are on your way upwards from Coping and are passing through.
Case 3: You are on your way down from Bounceback, and also passing through but trying to get back.

Whilst there are general characteristics of this state, some of what you can spot in yourself will depend on which of these three cases apply to you.

Case 1

Breakeven is an ok state. The key here is that if you've been here a long time and don't expect anything different, you may in fact create the conditions that ensure you remain exactly where you are.

Nothing will massively change, and there won't be a lot of capacity for high performance or success, but things will tick along. You'll feel stress quite often, not acutely or dangerously, but you will experience it. Your Coping mechanisms will have to kick in to help manage the stress. These will drain energy and leave you tired. You're likely to recover at some point, maybe with lower energy than normal, and climb back to just ticking along.

Case 2

Your resilience is on the way up, and you experience a new sense of surplus energy. It's like the snowdrops poking through the snow during winter. This is only good news; you are delighted! So you keep investing more in your resilience, whilst aware that your learning capability and this newfound surplus are fragile.

Case 3

You recognise you are at this level of resilience because of context; your situation has changed. You may have had experience of this before, and find it simple to accept it. You protect your resilience as much as possible. You know what helps your resilience: being present, energy, and perhaps connecting with your purpose as often as you can. You are more than surviving so you might feel blessed.

Cases 2 and 3 are transitory. Case 1 is chronic stuckness.

Middle of Breakeven: How do you know?

Here's the fast track.

Observable Behaviour	Satisfactory performance, but won't set the heather on fire
	Low expectations of change, can be cynical if stuck here
	Has limited perspective. In fact may not have seen what another way of living might look or feel like – may genuinely have no idea of another way
	Unlikely to step up to take responsibility unless very clearly part of role
	Will take on new stuff if within comfort zone. Change has to be forced if outside of comfort zone
	Will assert workload boundaries which is useful, but often in a manner that can be uppity. This comes about if feels somehow wronged
	Laughs stuff off
Internal Talk	That was a good day, nothing too difficult came up
	This is boring but I don't mind!
	This is not my bag, someone else can do it
	Strong use of 'them/us' in thinking, especially if in Case 1, chronic Coping. Eg 'They' always want something more. What do 'they' expect us to do, work weekends?!
	I like this work but if they ask for x-y-z, I don't know what I'll say
What You Feel	Satisfied enough, life's not bad
	Can feel stress, can feel fatigue but will move away and leave it

Relationship with Stress	Case 1: think they suffer from tremendous stress (but may not have any idea of what real negative stress is like)
	They don't really know the dangerous stress reaction unless they have witnessed it directly
Relationship with Change	Again?
	You wish!
Relationship with Control	I want to control the things I want to. But I'm not taking on anyone else's job!

Coping

When you are Coping, you are just managing what you need to do, versus the capacity you have. All your energy is spent on managing what is on your plate. You don't tell people that you feel completely flaky sometimes, you keep going. You have your wobbles, but you're on it, there is no way you are going to let it all slip. It'll be better tomorrow.

Often things take longer than you had anticipated which is frustrating, but you do put in additional hours when you need to. Otherwise sometimes things slip, or they are shoved out at whatever the quality. It doesn't make you feel so good, but that's life, and it's better that things get done.

Sometimes you make mistakes. That's the sign of being out of control and you absolutely hate that! You pull it back, you rein it in, you shift to cope better. Everything's back in the box.

To cope, you may disconnect from a whole lot of stuff, just to give yourself the possibility of surviving. You feel quite far away from feeling content or happy. You may miss the feeling of being relaxed, or the time to see friends or hang out with the family in an easy way. You are aware that not all of life is available to you and this sense haunts you a little. But you're pretty pleased just to survive… it could so easily be the other way. So for now, it's enough. You are Coping.

If Coping strategies are successfully stopping a shift to Fragmentation and Breakdown, Coping is a great place to be. But it's inherently rigid. Coping is a state where things are held as much as possible at status quo – no change!

Coping: How do you know?

Here's the fast track.

Observable Behaviour	Rushed, scatty, disorganised
	Tense quite often. Mood swings. Lack of real joy or sense of being relaxed
	'In yourself' – not reaching out as much
	Pushes back sometimes on stuff that is definitely in remit
	Keeps head down in meetings; aims to avoid either arguments or more work
	Uses language like 'I'll try' instead of 'I can' or 'I will'
	Can be moany
	Talks about tiredness often
	When prompted, laughs wryly about 'surviving'
	If in chronic Coping, will strongly resist change

Internal Talk	**About others**
	I can't believe they've asked me to do that as well, it's out of order
	Why can't they see that it's not possible?
	I just can't be bothered to argue
	To self
	I just need to get some more time to get on top of it all
	Life is such a juggle!
	How can I do this in the time I don't have?!
	Get a grip, come on, you can do this
What You Feel	Mental fatigue. Possible physical fatigue
	Often feels helpless
	There has to be another way
	And, initially in the face of any challenge, small or big – angry, maybe feels like crying, unable to see the wood from the trees, overwhelmed. Then forces a way back to a solution
	Over time, sense of hardening
Relationship with Stress	Always present and this is normal
	Can be overwhelmed by it sometimes, it can feel dangerous if out of control
	Needs to resist it
Relationship with Change	Incremental, within comfort zone only
	No capacity for any significant change
	May want the change, but can't enact it. May say 'yes' to doing something, but can't manage
Relationship with Control	Hates feeling of being out of control. Will work to get things back in control. May hold onto control to give sense of control. Or if control in one context not possible, may shift the urge for control to another context

Fragmentation

This is a state of breakup. Overall you feel unstable and unsafe. Every so often things are ok, but most often things are not ok. In work terms, this has a very strong impact on performance. In personal life, it can put relationships under extreme pressure.

You can experience deep Fragmentation. This is a dangerous long-term state, where someone has not been Coping for a long time, has lost sight of that, and is almost at Breakdown.

There is another kind of Fragmentation: when the person is not able to Cope in a stable way, and fluctuates between Fragmentation and Coping.

In Fragmentation you lose both perspective and energy. Perspective which is out of reach is needed to improve your Coping mechanisms. You will therefore suffer strongly from the negative effects of stress. It's not a state where you can trust your own judgement on what to do in this situation.

Early Fragmentation is the most difficult resilience state to spot; it is often hidden from the person and only observed through the eyes of others. It becomes apparent through inconsistency of behaviour and performance, plus conflicting emotions that overwhelm the person such as anger, fear, teariness, relief and confusion.

Those in Fragmentation are likely to strongly seek control. Fragmentation triggers control-freak behaviour and indeed having control becomes more important than the outcome of that control.

Fragmentation: How do you know?

Here's the fast track.

Observable Behaviour	Mood swings, mood is difficult to predict
	Prone to high irritancy, can blow up
	Tension
	Can be joyless
	Forceful, hard
Internal Talk	I can't stand this
	They are so out of order
	I hate this, I hate them
	I am so fed up with this
	This is so unfair
	I need to breathe
	I must get away
	I mustn't let my guard down
What You Feel	Mental fatigue, possibly physical fatigue
	Lonely
	That everything is reduced to a task, even seeing friends is a part of the to-do list
	Cynical
	There is no time
	Varying levels of anger, overwhelmedness, crying
	Forceful. Over time, you feel harder and harder. You may lose your softness

Relationship with Stress	Acutely high stress reaction, but it's so normalised that it's not really felt. Lost sight of normal
Relationship with Change	Change? That's a joke
Relationship with Control	I used to have it, but almost don't remember what that felt like

Breakdown – this is where the person cannot absorb any stress any more

This is an acute, time-limited psychiatric disorder that manifests primarily as a severe stress-induced depression, anxiety or dissociation. The person is no longer able to function on a day-to-day basis until the disorder is resolved. A mental Breakdown is defined by its temporary nature, and is closely tied to psychological burnout, severe overwork, sleep deprivation and similar stressors, which combine to temporarily overwhelm an individual with otherwise sound mental faculties. A mental Breakdown also shares many symptoms with the acute phase of post-traumatic stress disorder.

The major symptom of a mental Breakdown is depression. When someone is depressed they may experience weight gain, suicidal thoughts, or loss of interest in social, family, or work life. Another symptom of Breakdown is anxiety, which can produce an increase in blood pressure, dizziness, trembling, or feeling sick to the stomach. Panic attacks are very similar to mini breakdowns but can also be a symptom of a real Breakdown. Having a hard time breathing and extreme fear may occur in those who are experiencing a panic attack.

If the person is mildly depressed, many of the above symptoms will be felt. Confusion, erratic behaviour, loss of judgement, lack of sleep, low self-esteem, ill health and a breakdown of relationships are all common.

Breakdown: How do you know?

Here's the fast track.

Observable Behaviour	Weepy
	Listless
	Lost interest
	Sleeping a lot
Internal Talk	I can't think
	I'm so ashamed
	I feel guilt
	I can't go on
	I am such a failure
	I can't breathe
	I just don't know how to
	I don't know what they want
What You Feel	Sick
	Joyless
	Unable to move
	Lost
	Shame
	Guilt
	Lonely
	Useless
	A failure

Relationship with Stress	It doesn't matter
Relationship with Change	It doesn't matter
Relationship with Control	It doesn't matter. That's what other people have

The Resilient Way

The Resilient Way is based on two principles:

Principle 1

Understand and accept that resilience drives much of behaviour in work and life.

This is true for you and it's true for those around you, your team, your peers, your boss, your stakeholders, your family and friends.

Principle 2

You have to invest in resilience for it to extend, and indeed for it to remain at its current level. Without investment it will drop.

Embracing these principles is the ticket to crossing over the resilience 'gateway' mentioned in the Introduction.

To understand resilience means reading the resilience data of any situation. For this you need to invest in your skills of noticing and accepting.

Stories of Resilience

Look at these stories which illustrate the different levels of resilience across The Resilience Dynamic®. None of the stories represent real people, but all are based on real-life examples that have been put together to illustrate real ideas behind resilience. Each story has a different starting point. There is a map to guide you to which story might be of most interest to you.

Ian – at Breakthrough
Fiona – slipping from the middle of the Whoosh backwards
Des – on the Whoosh but bumped back into Bounceback
Elaine – gradually getting to Bounceback upwards after a failed relationship
Sylvia – stuck in Breakeven
Bill – aiming for Coping after Breakdown

Resilience Dynamic®
Resilience is our ability to reshape

Ian – at Breakthrough

Ian was head of Strategic Change Capability in a global services organisation. His service was one of the new and leading lights within the organisation. Ian was growing it quite specifically at a pace which he thought sustainable; it was a stretch but not too silly. He had a good team of people, some hand-chosen. And good clients. The team trusted one another, debated like mad, and got on with delivery whenever the decisions were made. His guys were pushing the boat out on one particular methodology to enable adaptability in global organisations; it seemed to be going down well. Ian left them to lead all of that, whilst his job was about creating the brand both internally and externally. It was demanding, he was always on show, and whilst he was good at it, he needed to be quiet as a counterbalance. Difficult to find quiet time, he had invested personally in a boat, and could take off at weekends and completely cut off. Bliss.

Ian was doing something he genuinely loved. He was a high performer in work, and outside in his personal life. He had great friends, a great family with good relationships. Of course not without their ups and downs, but good. At home, he was open and honest, and when he really needed to, would really lean on his family. He had had a cancer scare in recent times, had come through, but had completely sought support from his loved ones around him. He was grateful for this, and for the chance to keep going. He was a good communicator, and sought to know himself and his foibles well. He accepted most, although some were becoming an annoyance to him now, and he was tackling them head on.

One of these was how busy he seemed to be. He would help in many of the domains connected to his core purpose, which was about enabling organisations to be great places. He saw organisations as a critical part of any individual's wellbeing, and their culture and outlook critical to the individual's success in life. His mission was to help improve this. It meant taking quite a challenging line in the marketplace, but what was more challenging was taking that stance internally. Was his organisation really set up for the best wellbeing of its staff? Ian knew not. So his line was to navigate between what was necessary for his clients who were often easier to work with, and go steady, slowly and positively, internally to change the culture around him.

From the outside, Ian could be seen as a go-to person for help, ideas, drive and delivery against his area of expertise of strategic change. He would aim to help anyone who came in under that domain, although was ruthless about sticking to this and not being side-lined into other related areas.

One of Ian's biggest learnings from that time was how brilliant it was to depend on others, and how this had increased his outlook on all aspects of his life. This was somehow part of the solution to his busyness – he could lean on others even more to enable change. Another thing he had learnt was just not to get so caught up in work. He now had his own boat, loved sailing and also being deliberately cut off from work at weekends. Despite the growing culture in the organisation to jump onto emails on Sundays, Ian was entirely calm about drawing very clear boundaries between the time he committed to his home and work life. It didn't mean he separated his mind into two parts, but he did divide his time very clearly.

ᴗ The Resilience Lens

o   What levels of resilience are demonstrated here?
o   What shifts in resilience are there? What underlies the shift – is it externally or internally driven?
o   What does this person do that drains their resilience?
o   What does this person do to enhance their resilience?

Fiona – slipping from the middle of the Whoosh backwards

Fiona's situation was intriguing. She was a very high performer, well liked and well regarded in her workplace. Proud of the life she had created – a good family life, a good work life, comfortable. Not all completely perfect, but Fiona was a pragmatist and didn't expect it all to be rose-tinted. Far from it, she seemed to relish in the gnarliness of life; she was a great problem solver.

Fiona was married, with two kids in their late teens/early twenties. One had already moved out of the family home into student accommodation, the other was finishing off their final year at school. Her husband was a contract project engineer in the oil industry, happy in his job, a very steady partner. He didn't bring work issues home with him, so Fiona kept the lines really tight also and never discussed work at home. They had a good relationship, enjoyed the company of a few close friends who still lived nearby, and had great holidays together walking in the Alps and practising their German.

Fiona made quite a few sacrifices for work. Whilst keeping her long-standing promise to come home in time for dinner, she would log on later in the evenings to clear email. She'd do the same on a Sunday. She thought this acceptable for her level: she had a very large staff of hundreds of people, the job was hugely operational and could throw anything up at any time. The business depended on her and she always delivered. So it was a busy and good life.

However, Fiona had a sense of a growing discontentment. Despite being well regarded, she seemed to be doing the same things again and again in her career, and was losing her motivation to continue in the same vein. She was bored. What an admission, it didn't seem right! So she tried her best to ignore it. Not least because what other options did she have? Fiona had expected promotion two years ago but had been told she still needed to demonstrate senior leadership capability in her current role.

Fiona felt stuck. She was stuck doing something really well that she no longer felt fulfilled in. She couldn't move up. She hadn't really talked to friends about it, and only a little at home. The biggest issue for her was the fear of facing the real issue of what would give her meaning day to day. It seemed such a difficult question.

She found she was increasingly narky at home, and sometimes in work although she did a good job at hiding it. She felt sometimes a bit unstable. And she was feeling low in motivation – so much to do operationally in work, and her people could really fulfil it, but were looking to her to continue to set direction. Fiona's resilience was slipping, and she was moving from the middle of the Whoosh down to Bounceback, where her energies were more and more up and down.

Fiona's reclaim to her resilience would take some hard self-evaluation and looking at the areas she was so determined to keep the lid on.

↻ The Resilience Lens

o   What levels of resilience are demonstrated here?
o   What shifts in resilience are there? What underlies the shift – is it externally or internally driven?
o   What does this person do that drains their resilience?
o   What does this person do to enhance their resilience?

Des – between on the Whoosh and bumped back into Bounceback

Des enjoyed a position as a senior middle manager in a very large public organisation. He was part of the realm of the senior management cohort that was consulted by the senior leaders of the organisation. He ran a very good ship, had introduced some of the leading new thinking in terms of performance management into his domain, and got some good payback as a result. A good salary, a decent pension and quite a few good jollies.

The work intellectually stimulated Des although it was hugely demanding in terms of his time and energy. Although his direct team was small, he had real influence with many of the local institutions involved in his field, and his time was often taken up with visiting, consulting and cajoling, and importantly, hosting the CEO conference for all the local institutions.

Des enjoyed a direct line to the CEO of the organisation because of the leading work he was doing. For several years the work had been growing in the background: a systemic change involving a power shift, happening gradually. Des knew a lot about it and knew a structural change was coming soon. Indeed he had sorted his own patch out to be ready for the change, he had a good team, his partnership principles were good. He felt ready to head up the new role for the new combined structure. His area had enjoyed being one of the best practice sites quoted in all of the national debate and he felt confident in his future. He was often in the limelight and whilst his boss often muscled in on this, Des still felt he was known in the right places for the new top job that would come out of the restructure.

His personal life could have been better really. He was divorced now – maybe in the end work had taken its toll on their marriage. He had three kids, one of whom was currently staying with him whilst they finished their university exams. He had a good relationship with his kids, although he hadn't really been around them so much when they were younger, and they all tended to lean on their mother for the emotional stuff. Des was there for activities, holidays and money. Oh, more than that, but sometimes that's what it felt like. Des didn't have a long-term partner, but enjoyed seeing his girlfriend quite often. It was a mutual arrangement, not to see one another too often – it worked for them both because of their work demands. Maybe once he got a bit more time, he would invest in changing it to be more.

Des was unexpectedly unsuccessful in his application for the new top job of running the combined partnerships. Des couldn't understand at all, he had done so much, why was he overlooked for an outsider? He had had feedback that his delivery capability was unquestionable, but the interview panel had all felt they had needed fresh blood to lead the new institutes that would be formed as a result of restructure.

Des felt totally disenfranchised. In Des's own words, before the interviews, he had been somewhere on the Whoosh, not at Breakthrough by any means, but in his view, he had been pretty good. But his recent failure to get the new job had been a shock.

His resilience, built on his old context, didn't seem to offer him much support in this new context.

↻ The Resilience Lens

o   What levels of resilience are demonstrated here?
o   What shifts in resilience are there? What underlies the shift – is it externally or internally driven?
o   What does this person do that drains their resilience?
o   What does this person do to enhance their resilience?

Elaine – gradually getting to Bounceback after a failed relationship

Elaine was a high performer who enjoyed much of her life. Part of a European team enabling major change within a global organisation, she got the chance to live abroad, travel to all the main capitals in Europe, work with many different nationalities, and soak up the atmosphere of the places she visited. It was challenging work, but she loved a challenge, and especially if she could live in one of the best places in Europe, Madrid. She could speak fluent Spanish, enjoyed the lifestyle and weather when she could, and altogether relished the opportunity. She felt glamorous because her life seemed glamorous.

Elaine was in her late 30s, and although had a nice set of friends in Madrid, wasn't with a partner. She had had boyfriends but they just didn't meet her ideas of what she was looking for. She imagined a similarly glamorous life somewhere, with good looks, good food and good wine all included. It wasn't at all easy meeting someone; she never seemed to have much time. So when she had met someone on a plane that seemed, well, brilliant, she had fallen straight into a mega relationship with them. They were based in the UK, but often travelled to Spain, and so the two of them started a long-distance relationship. Elaine fell hook, line and sinker, and started to discuss commitment and making the relationship real.

This is when it started to go wrong. Instead of waiting to see how things panned out, Elaine had decided to fly into the UK as a surprise and propose a living-together solution as a test before going the next step. She had got a nasty shock when on arrival at her partner's home address she saw two kids in the garden, and her partner with another woman. He was married.

Elaine was devastated. Her return to Madrid should have involved a week in serious venture negotiations. She should have been clear-headed. But she was weeping all the time, overwhelmed with the feeling of being lied to, of losing her dream, of being alone. She was also embarrassed, appalled at herself for being so stupid, and altogether confused. She phoned her boss on the Monday and managed, whilst weeping, to explain that she had split up from whom she thought she was going to marry, and she couldn't come to work that week. Her boss said ok, but she knew it was all a bit rubbish. What would they think of her in work?

Elaine decided to fly home and lean on her parents and family. For a week she did little except sleep, talk, drink tea, and get mollycoddled by her folks. And in the middle of that Elaine had realised how many things had not been right in the relationship, and how desperate she had been for it to work. She had let herself be very exploited. She had held herself accountable to a promise she'd made that was on a false understanding. She was learning that she shouldn't be bound by promises that turned out to be bad for her.

Elaine reconnected with a part of herself from home, a good part, that she liked. It was more homely, more simple than her glam life. Elaine had started to address what she wanted truly out of life.

It took Elaine a long time to fully assimilate all that. But she bounced back from the relationship failure quite quickly. It was like a whole set of screens had been lifted from her eyes: not only about the partner, but also about herself. She had a much clearer perspective of herself. Rebuilding her life was a long-term matter, but the trauma of the failure was a real wake-up call for Elaine in her life, and she set about putting things onto a more real footing.

The Resilience Lens

o   What levels of resilience are demonstrated here?
o   What shifts in resilience are there? What underlies the shift – is it externally or internally driven?
o   What does this person do that drains their resilience?
o   What does this person do to enhance their resilience?

Sylvia – stuck in Breakeven

Sylvia was a mum of three kids and worked part-time as a staff nurse which she loved. The hours gave her enough time to run around and do all the kids and house things, and still do something for herself.

Sylvia managed quite fine, but always had a story to tell of some drama or other. It was often with the same people: the local health clinic who were just a total waste of time; the local community hall that insisted on noise every Friday night with their disco; the primary school where the teachers just didn't really understand her kids so well; one or two of the neighbours who parked their cars too near their house.

A lot of the drama was outside of work, and work was a bit more stable. She knew what she was about, and she prided herself on quality care. She wasn't one of the ones that ignored patients to do their paperwork. She did what was right, so what if she didn't complete all the paperwork? Sylvia had had an issue at the hospital with a case where the drugs issued to a particular older patient hadn't been documented and the patient ended up with a double dose. It hadn't been her fault really, it was all about workload and them not understanding at all that the system was very slow and she had run out of time. It was an easy mistake to make, not life-threatening for anyone. And the patient was ok, well, had had a bit of a dip, but in the end was fine. She had chosen to more or less ignore the issue and just put her head down.

She loved being in a hospital, and the banter and support from her colleagues. The drugs case issue had left a bit of an overhang with some of them, but she had her mates who had backed her up, and in the end there had been a review of working hours versus supervisory staff in the ward. Well, what a hoo-ha, and the new structure seemed not to make one iota of a difference to Sylvia. But at least her case had been part of the trigger for something they were trying to do.

Even with all that, she liked her job and wanted to do well in it.

Sylvia coped with the ups and downs of life, often by moaning about them to her mates, but in the end she got through and back on a more even keel. Nothing much changed, but in a way that was what she liked and she put quite a lot of effort into making sure that things didn't change. In times of change, however, Sylvia struggled to cope, and did her best to resist change.

Sylvia wasn't a high performer, and in fact her performance was at best satisfactory but often mediocre. She didn't take responsibility for the drugs case issue that had arisen, and had instead got in union help in case she was threatened in any way. Sylvia's resistance to change and not taking responsibility meant she was seen as a liability in her workplace; she was a potential for being offered redundancy. Sylvia didn't know that's what other people thought, and would have been shocked to discover that.

☺ The Resilience Lens

○ What levels of resilience are demonstrated here?

○ What shifts in resilience are there? What underlies the shift – is it externally or internally driven?

○ What does this person do that drains their resilience?

○ What does this person do to enhance their resilience?

Bill – aiming for Coping after Breakdown

Bill was allocated a coach to assist in his return to work after a period off work from 'stress'. Bill had in fact had a mini breakdown and was now expected to be coming back to work, within the same performance conditions as he had experienced during his breakdown. Bill was a senior leader in his organisation, and responsible for one of the newer business units which was set up in partnership with another organisation.

The commissioning conversation for the coaching with the CEO was all about coming back to work successfully and in good health. The coach was to help him understand how to do that. There was no doubt that the new business partnership had to succeed and the whole thing was in the spotlight. This included dealing with the press.

Bill had been off for several months. He was an intelligent, savvy and practical man, who seemed both embarrassed and angry at his breakdown. He was used to succeeding, he was known for his delivery capability. In his mind he had been the scapegoat for a bullying situation that had arisen that he had not handled well – the bully had got away with it but he, Bill, had had to leave because of his performance.

When the coach met him, Bill was still massively affected by the bullying and the trauma. He was cautious, tired, erratic, sometimes compliant, sometimes argumentative, and overall seemed vulnerable. He had a muddled view on the situation in his work and his role, particularly around trusting the leaders of the partner institution. And he was very muddled as to what had caused his breakdown in the first place. He understood what had been the symptoms – taking on more and more because it all seemed important, low performance, muddled thinking and decision making, a loss of confidence from others around him, and overworking and exhaustion. Finally he was sent by his workplace to the doctors who signed him off sick. He was equally muddled about how he was when the coach met him – on the one hand saying he was fine, recovered, but on the other, emotional and distracted. He wasn't yet sleeping and seemed in an unhealthy state.

The work using the lens of the Resilience Dynamic® model helped Bill to recognise where he had been, that he had been at Breakdown. This was big news to start off with. It started the process of him accepting the whole thing. In seeing this clearly it did help him recognise that to get to Coping was a good target. This defined the work very clearly for the coaching.

The idea of shooting for high performance was entirely inappropriate in this case.

↻ The Resilience Lens

o   What levels of resilience are demonstrated here?
o   What shifts in resilience are there? What underlies the shift – is it externally or internally driven?
o   What does this person do that drains their resilience?
o   What does this person do to enhance their resilience?

The Bottom Line

This chapter has set out clearly and simply the different dimensions for each resilience level: observable behaviour, the kinds of inner talk that might be going on, and the relations to stress, change and control.

The purpose of this chapter is to ensure clarity so that you understand how to spot different resilience levels in yourself and in others around you. It's extremely helpful if you are in a support role. It is essential if you are in a management or leadership level.

Stories are used to illustrate how resilience might manifest itself during transitions, movement or indeed stuck resilience states.

Chapter 7

More Resilience = Less Stress

*'I'm less stressed than two years ago.
I've hugely grown up.'*

Alternative view

Say 'no'. You are saying 'yes' to something else.

Chapter Overview

This chapter sets out to explain what stress is, and how resilience acts as a buffer to the negative stress reaction. The chapter explains three phases of the stress reaction, which illustrate the tipping point between positive versus negative stress.

The chapter will help you understand:

o   the difference between the stress reaction and stressors
o   the different phases of the stress reaction and the implications
o   how the two main hormones of adrenalin and cortisol create impact in your mind and body
o   how these hormones interrupt your normal circadian rhythms.

The Resilience Scene

More than 300 million people – nearly 5% of the world's population – suffer from clinical depression or anxiety. In the USA, it is much higher, with nearly 20% of the population reporting suffering from anxiety-related disorders.

The Gallop 2018 Emotions Report, which surveys across 146 countries, shows that world happiness is at its lowest level since the survey was started in 2006. The World Health Organization estimates that depression and anxiety will match cardiovascular diseases as the world's largest major health disorders by 2020.

Young people are increasingly vulnerable, suffering from Social Anxiety Disorder, the new phenomenon of loneliness and anxiety linked to social media.

AT Kearney Global Business Policy Council
Year-Ahead Predictions 2019

It's a disaster, this whole thing. The lack of resilience is costing us a lot, in both treatment costs (estimated as $1 trillion), in lost productivity (no estimate of financial impact), and importantly, the whole tragedy of people missing joy and satisfaction in their life.

And as we described in the Introduction of the book, The Resilience Engine sees a slip backwards in our resilience levels, from what was once 'ok' to Coping and indeed not coping. In a recent survey 82% of respondents said that the demand for resilience was high, and 44% said it was high and rising. Only 10% surveyed said it was manageable.

Coping and not coping, or what we call 'Fragmentation'. Two resilience states. Neither state has sufficient resilience for driving change. But change is upon us and change is what we need.

If ever there was a time that we needed to invest in our resilience, it's now.

What Is Stress?

Stress. So often talked and written about.

The term was stolen and adapted from physics, where the force of a strain, ie stress placed upon a physical object, will cause it to bend, misshape and potentially break. Since this first definition, there has been a plethora of literature about it and how to manage it.

There is good stress. The stuff that gets you up in the morning, the alarm that rings or the dog barking; you need to get out of bed and your response is positive. Or when you are just about to address a large conference, when you experience a combination of excitement and nerves. Or speaking out in a meeting when nervous and feeling really great that you did, because it changed the course of the decisions made. All the 'good' stress is serving that kick of adrenalin you need to respond well, to lift your performance.

There is bad stress. Those who are suffering badly from the bad stuff will just find the idea of good stress ridiculous, even patronising.

You will have experienced bad stress. When your mind can't focus. When you have physical signs of tension – headaches, stiff shoulders and back, an upset stomach. They're the early indicators. However, the deeper, more worrying reactions include your head really not feeling right, when you are unable to make decisions, or health-impacting hyper tension, depression or anxiety. These are the longer-term indicators. It's when your mind and body are hijacked and you can't seem to get away.

The word 'stress' is bandied around all the time. It has been quoted several times as the 'Health Epidemic of our age' apparently by the World Health Organisation (although the exact original is untraceable). It can even be worn like a badge of honour in certain contexts.

But it's such a flabby word.

There are two separate things:

Stressors

Those triggers or stimuli in life that require a lift in your response, mental and physical, to enable you to act appropriately.

Stressors can be events, people, environments that an individual considers demanding or challenging and that threaten in some way the individual's sense of safety. Within this broad definition, there are absolute stressors and relative stressors.[69,70] Absolute stressors are those triggers or stimuli that everyone would interpret as stress-inducing. They include universal events such as earthquakes, terrorist attacks etc. Relative stressors are those triggers or stimuli which are subjective, and trigger different reactions in different people. They include pressures at work, traffic whilst driving, sitting an exam.

Stress

This is the response to stressors whereby stress hormones – adrenalin and cortisol – are released. This can be described using the term 'General Adaptation System' which works like this:

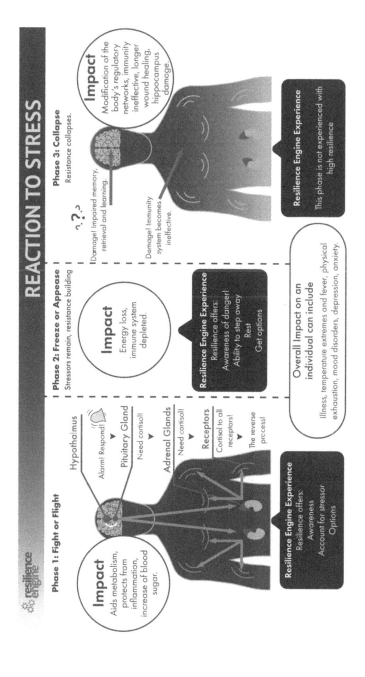

Phase 1: Initial alarm reaction

Context	Alarm sounded, something is going to be bad/unsafe, you need to decide what to do quickly
Stress reaction purpose	To trigger appropriate reaction to the stressor – fight or flight
Stress hormones released	Adrenalin & cortisol
Impact of stress hormones	All the good stuff! o Aids the metabolism of fat, protein, carbohydrates o Protects the body from inflammation o Increases blood sugar o Suppresses the immune system to release energy so that the system of receptors can be activated and the cortisol can do its binding work to them. (Translation: if you need to run away from danger, the body is activating acute energy into your legs, hips and feet so you can leg it!) o Works with adrenalin to create memories of short-term emotional events; the body's mechanism to help us to remember to avoid the stressor in future

Phase 2: Resistance

Context	The same stressors remain, so you resist the stressor
Stress reaction purpose	To keep up the appropriate reaction to the stressor – fight or flight
Stress hormones released	Continued release of adrenalin and cortisol. The level of stress hormone in the body becomes normalised
Impact of stress hormones	Your body is working hard to fight the stressor o Continued energy loss o Continued impediment to immune system full functioning o A new learnt way of handling stress: freeze or appease

Phase 3: Collapse

Context	Long-term exposure to the stressor. Resistance is reduced and collapses
Stress reaction purpose	Depletion. Signal to get away from stressor
Impact of stress hormones	The bad side of stress o Modification of the body's regulatory networks o Immune system becomes ineffective o Lengthening of wound-healing time o Reduces bone formation o Hippocampus damage; impairs memory retrieval and learning Overall impact on an individual can include o Illness o Temperature extremes and fever o Physical exhaustion o Mood disorders o Depression o Anxiety o Fear o Pain

You may think that cortisol is an unhelpful hormone, but it's not! The hormone isn't produced solely in response to stress; chronic stress just puts it into overdrive. Normal levels are critical for maintaining steady energy throughout the day. And cortisol orchestrates the performance of other key hormones, like oestrogen, testosterone and thyroid.

Cortisol is your friend in many situations. You need a steady stream of cortisol to function at all – it is in fact secreted in a steady state way across what is called our circadian rhythm.[71,72] A healthy curve begins with cortisol levels highest in the morning. Cortisol levels are normally lowest around 3 a.m., then begin to rise, peaking around 8 a.m:

The Cortisol Curve

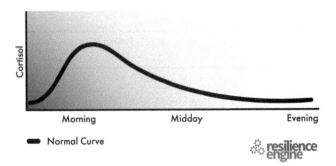

What a lovely, easy curve!

That feels quite different from these curves, all signs of the negative stress reaction:

The Cortisol Curve

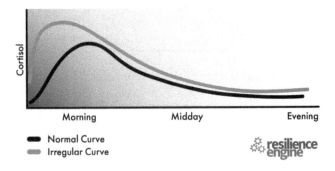

Cortisol rockets too early

If you routinely wake up in the early hours of the morning feeling buzzed or indeed anxious, your cortisol has kicked in because your brain is demanding that you deal with stuff now! You may notice that you rarely sleep, your mind races from the moment you wake up, and you might be edgy in the morning. What's more, you'll run out of steam around mid-morning.

Depletion of energy or an acute worry are the underlying causes of this.

The Cortisol Curve

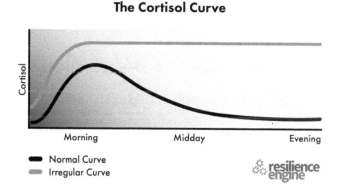

Overload

Too much caffeine, lack of carbs throughout the day, or just sheer dogged intensity. If cortisol levels stay high, you'll feel wired but tired. You may feel like you're always racing to catch up and you have the go-go-go sense and you talk quickly. You will suffer brain fog and get easily irritated. You will become inefficient. If this happens daily, you'll start to lose your enthusiasm for life.

Often this is caused by a combination of workload levels being beyond capacity plus ignoring your energy needs.

The Cortisol Curve

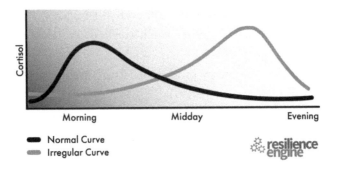

Cortisol

Morning   Midday   Evening

● Normal Curve
● Irregular Curve

resilience engine

Rock 'n' roll in the evening

If you are buzzed in conversation at night, or you train at the gym in the evenings, it's likely that your cortisol levels are shooting up in the evening, contrary to the normal circadian rhythm. You will find you are restless in the evenings and distract yourself by going online or exercise, you will worry more in the evenings, and falling asleep takes ages.

This is where your rhythm is being hijacked; your activity is making cortisol slow-down impossible.

The Cortisol Curve

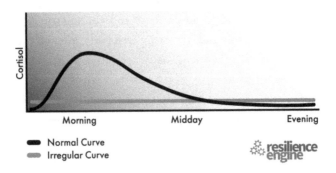

Cortisol

Morning   Midday   Evening

● Normal Curve
● Irregular Curve

resilience engine

Exhaustion

After cortisol has been elevated for an extended period, it can drop off completely. This signals adrenal exhaustion, when the overworked glands have shut down. You feel like you're dragging yourself along, even after sleep. Any spike through the likes of exercise feels good but doesn't last. You may keep falling asleep during the day.

This may be caused by prolonged lack of physical and mental rest and/or sleep, in combination with the prolonged stress reaction of cortisol overdrive.

Conclusions so far

○ Good stress, or rather the steady secretion of cortisol into our system, is necessary for everything we do in life. It's good!

○ Alarm stress, the sudden hike of cortisol release in response to a threat, is in fact really useful if (a) it's in response to a real threat and (b) you are in a position to act on the primal fight or flight.

○ Alarm stress is not good – it is bad – if it has been a reaction that is unnecessary to a stressor or set of stressors, where the stressors don't merit the full system being hijacked. It's an unnecessary strain on the system.

○ Long-term bad stress is bad.

Resilience and stress

The more resilience in your system, the more you can choose your reaction to stressors.

That means you can choose not to feel the negative stress reaction. Kelly McGonigal's[73-76] work on stress shows exactly this: those that believe they will get 'stressed' do indeed experience negative stress; those that don't don't.

That's it. That's the nub of it.

Think about that. You choose the reaction in the moment. How can you be resourced to make this choice? You need to build the foundations for your resilience so that your reactions in any context can be open, thoughtful, appropriate and honouring what you need. That all leads to not experiencing the bad side of stress. You proact in order to react well:

Proact to **React** intentionally

Proactively, you need to work out what your intention is within a relationship, meeting, event or long-term project. Your proactive reflection on this, together with a plan of how to support that intention, will mean that even in a heated moment or exchange, you can draw on that intention and react to support it. Any release of adrenalin and cortisol is performance-enhancing and not bad-stress inducing.

Being resilient doesn't mean you don't step outside of your comfort zone, where stressors are at play. Actually the opposite! But you don't have to experience the negative stress reaction.

The Resilient Way

There are two parts to developing your resilience as a buffer to stress.

The first is to understand your barriers to resilience. In doing this you will extend your resilience potential, releasing and letting go of the things that hold your resilience back. The top barriers discovered through The Resilience Engine's research are within this chapter.

The second is to put more into the resilience bank every day. This is the work of supporting your Adaptive Capacity[23] discussed in Chapter 4. Part 3 of the book introduces the Top Enablers of resilience.

From The Resilience Engine's research, there are three out of the many barriers to resilience that really stand out. These cause bad stress.

o   The person has weak or no boundaries, and where this happens, they don't feel secure.
o   They overestimate their capacity and end up busy, busy, busy.
o   They have a do-it-yourself driver that means they don't ask for help.

(✐) **Write down**

See below for how these fit together and the kinds of drivers that create the barrier.

Circle those that you notice in yourself the most.

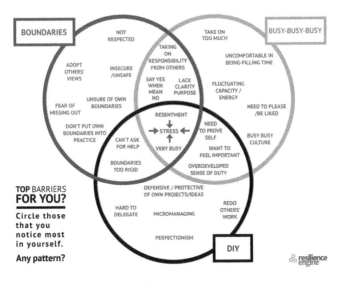

Source: Diagram produced by Alison Kane, Director of Services, Resilience Engine. All copyright reserved.

This tool is part of the Resilient Manager Toolkit service from The Resilience Engine. See http://www.resilienceengine.com/ our-services/ for further information.

🔍 Review

Do you notice any pattern in those you have circled?

Top barrier 1: Weak boundaries

Healthy boundaries are all about you first knowing what you need to be 'ok', then asserting that within the situation. As Brené Brown[77] says:

> *Daring to set boundaries is about having the courage to love ourselves, even when we risk disappointing others. We can't base our own worthiness on others' approval... Only when we believe, deep down, that we are enough can we say 'Enough!'*

162

Setting a boundary is when you have a clear 'line' that you don't want others to cross or you will feel uneasy, maybe disappointed in yourself, or, worse, violated in some way. That unsafe feeling might come out in terms of shame, guilt or anger.

Boundaries show up all across the Resilience Dynamic®. They show up especially when you are at Coping, or indeed not coping. Often there are deep-rooted patterns in your behaviour that allow others to walk across your safety lines, and you feel bad as a result. Since you haven't faced the truth of what you need, or indeed because your resilience is so low, you don't assert what you need.

You need boundaries in all areas of your life, from how you are next to people at a bus stop, to how you handle power in work, through to your intimate relationships with your partner. They matter in everything.

Physical boundaries are about ensuring that you are physically safe. You don't let a total stranger be really close to you at that bus stop!

You shift away, signalling a boundary of 'no closer!'

Within groups and organisations, there can be a culture of hugging that may not suit you but that you feel you have to adopt to fit in. What do you do? If it's not for you, when someone hugs you, you will feel at the minimum uneasy, but potentially you could suffer from the stress reaction that may mean you end up freezing – you end up stuck between wanting to tell someone to 'get off!' versus fitting in. In this 'freeze' mode, you are not yourself, you don't feel at ease, people in the group don't see you properly. They think you're quiet and possibly uninteresting. If only you could feel relaxed! All because of the hug issue.

Emotional boundaries are about ensuring that someone isn't holding power over you through undue pressure, or expectation or requirement. What does 'undue' mean? It's personal. Two people can act quite differently when faced with the same situation. Take the boss who is demanding. You keep capitulating to every demand because you find the boss intimidating. But your colleague, who has an easier relationship with them, manages to push back without too much hassle, and their workload is more manageable. Why can't it be the same for you? Your reaction is different, and somehow you are freezing. This annoys you, so you end up holding anger inside. Resentment grows.

This is a boundary issue. What is it about the way you see the boss that allows you to render yourself unresourceful, unable to ask for what you need, or at least to find a solution that will work for you both? Maybe it's been a pattern with others in authority in your life.

What do you imagine might happen if you said 'I can't' or 'I wonder if there's another way', or 'Can I do this later after x-y-z'? Often the reaction will be positive, especially if your intention is positive.

Your own set of beliefs and values both about the world and about yourself are at play here. You may fear setting a boundary because you imagine it to be worse than the consequence of letting someone walk over you. You don't try to set the boundary, you capitulate. Yet setting a boundary is often as simple as stating what you need, and asking if others can work to that. If they can, most often they will!

Of course there are times when their response is not positive, or at least it's difficult. Your need may be in conflict with someone else's needs. In personal situations, marriage or partnership, the give and take required to happily accommodate both parties' needs is enormous.

Being clear on what your boundaries are and asking others to respect them is a key part of your resilience. In the course of developing your resilience, you may discover that there are some situations, or some kinds of people, that you just no longer want to be with. Stopping is healthy boundary management.

When your resilience is high and you are choiceful about what you do and who you decide to be with, you will move nearer to thriving. Your relationships will be meaningful, and will give you energy back. This feels fabulous.

Top barrier 2: Busy-busy-busy

Being busy-busy-busy is so seductive. You feel good because you get things done. You feel good because people need you.

It is often the domain of those with Bounceback resilience. If your resilience is this kind of level, it's about balance. Too little activity and boredom can set in. Too much activity and overwhelm can set in. Too much activity again and again surpasses overwhelm and can lead to real fatigue. It's tough to achieve balance. Adrenalin, running around your system, can feel uplifting and energising. But trade on this too much, and you will deplete your body, leading to boom and bust.

You might end up feeding your body with caffeine or sugar to keep going. Leading to – yes, you guessed it, more boom and bust. (See earlier in the chapter for the associated cortisol curves.)

Or you might just end up feeling so tired that you don't sleep well. Your brain doesn't have sufficient capacity for dealing with everything you are cramming into it during the day, but it keeps trying, even in the middle of the night.

Or you can't think straight. Your subconscious (or your prefrontal cortex in fact), whilst operating incredibly efficiently around everything you throw at it, goes into a bit of meltdown, it temporarily shuts down. It means you can't close off one thing before another thing opens, and it all gets muddled up. The result is brain fog.

You might just have lost the habit of stopping. You're so attuned to being active, to getting onto the next thing, that it's really hard resting in between being busy. Instead of on-off, you are on-on.

Being busy-busy-busy destroys your resilience in the following ways:

o   Energy loss through all the juggle
o   Energy loss because you don't finish things well and lose the sense of satisfaction
o   Lost perspective on what's important
o   Which in turn means everything is deemed urgent and you end up doing non-important stuff
o   And you add more onto your plate…

What lies behind being busy-busy-busy?

This is the question to hold. What is it that drives the busy-busy-busy? There are three possibilities within The Resilience Engine's research findings:

o   You may be hooked on a vision of yourself that you are a superhero, and able to work miracles. Maybe because you achieve so much, people ask you to do it often. You love the praise. You love the adrenalin rush that comes from being so much in demand. People tell you that you work miracles and that feels good. And they ask again and again.

166

Please note, all superwomen out there, this is definitely for you!

Or

o You're a bit of a martyr. You rescue others, and in doing so, end up doing their tasks for them. Because you can, and you find it really difficult if others are uncomfortable. You take on their burden.

Or

o You are hooked on being needed, or being liked, or both. It's a special case of a boundary issue: you are avoiding saying 'no' in case you're not liked as a result. By saying 'yes' you overburden yourself and unnecessarily drain your resilience.

You are probably destroying your immune system. Professor of Organisational Psychology at the University of Lancaster Cary Cooper says leisure sickness usually happens to people in really pressurised jobs.

> *Your immune system is stimulated by the pressure, so when you have deadlines your body knows you can't get ill. When you take a break your immune system just thinks – no more pressure. I can get sick now.*[78,79]

When your resilience is at Coping or indeed for many in Bounceback, you won't see clearly the meaning or energy you personally will get out of all this busyness. Instead you will remain hijacked by your own hook. And you will do more, and get more tired, which runs the risk of further fatigue and resentment. You risk shifting towards Fragmentation, which is health-impacting. It's a vicious spiral.

🔍 **Review**

o   Investing in resilience means figuring out your sources of energy for real.

o   What activities give you energy back?

o   When you are at a higher level of resilience, you will be doing more of what you genuinely love. It doesn't mean it's all easy, but it will return some of the energy used up in the process. See Chapter 9, 'Top Enablers of Resilience', for more on energy.

Top barrier 3: Do It Yourself

This is one of the most debated barriers to resilience. You may come from a culture that applauds the hero who punches through things.

The lone rider.
The hero soldier.
The winner of the race.
The pioneering Chief Executive.

Always behind the scenes there is a team of folk who helped that person, but it's the hero that gets the glory.

You need sometimes to be a hero. It's up to you, and you alone, to figure things out, whatever the situation. For many high performers, the idea even of admitting that you don't know what to do and asking for others' input is an anathema. It's not cool. It's not right.

Your resilience requires you to be able to be independent. Of course! But The Resilience Engine research shows that being able to choose in any one situation how independent versus dependent you are leads to the highest success. You need to be able to be dependent on others too. Indeed you need to be able to be vulnerable. As Brené Brown says:

> *Vulnerability sounds like truth and feels like courage. Truth and courage aren't always comfortable, but they're never weakness.*[77]

Being able to choose whether you go down the independent or dependent route in any situation relies on muscles for both; you need to be able to switch on either one of them at any time. For you DIYers, it means tuning up those muscles of asking for help.

Those with the highest resilience work to ensure their drivers for independence and dependence are in balance and they continue to invest in stretching both. High-resilience leaders and managers invest in their Adaptive Capacity by proactively getting perspective regularly via others and stepping into different situations. That is not a DIY way of living. The bottom line for them is that in any one situation, they will choose whether they go down the DIY path, or call out for help, or both. They are flexible to do that, even in the face of challenge.

Applying the Resilient Way

Boundaries

© The Resilience Engine 2019

🔍 **Review**

Look at the following ten reasons to have healthy boundaries.

1.	**You're more self-aware**	There is a healthy separation between your own thoughts and feelings, and those of others
2.	**You become a better friend and partner**	People with less effective limits or boundaries are more likely to violate the boundaries of others too
3.	**You take better care of yourself**	It makes you more effective and less burned out. You can help others more effectively also
4.	**You're less stressed**	Without a boundary, you absorb the stress that exists around you and get drained
5.	**You're a better communicator**	Expressing your own needs in a clear and concise way avoids misunderstandings
6.	**You build more trust**	Communicating your own limits shows others that you are open, and that you trust them with your needs
7.	**You're less angry**	You don't experience violation so much, so there is less need for anger and resentment
8.	**You learn to say 'no'**	Not only less anger and resentment, but you gain your time back!
9.	**You do things you want to do**	You feel great because you're able to focus on the important things in life that give you energy
10.	**You become a more understanding person**	As Brené Brown[77] says: *'The most compassionate people I have interviewed as part of my work have been the most boundaried'*

Source: This tool is part of the Build Resilience Habits service from The Resilience Engine. See http://www.resilienceengine.com/our-services/ for further information.

(🖊) **Write down**

Circle the reasons which are most attractive for you.

Which out of these is the one you want to invest in? Double or triple circle this one!

✍ Change

For your top reason to invest in healthy boundaries, consider specifically what, where and with whom you want to change.

What boundaries will help you make this change?

What is your first step to creating or re-creating this boundary?

✔ Commit

Who will help you maintain your boundaries in a healthy way? Consider the Top Enablers of resilience in Chapter 9.

Busy-busy-busy

© The Resilience Engine 2019

🔍 Review

Consider these questions:

Do you find yourself saying 'yes' to a tonne of stuff, then regretting it later?

Are you committed to certain work projects or things outside of work that are fundamentally not interesting to you?

Are you doing things that are someone else's responsibility?

Do you beat yourself up about saying 'yes' because you have been trying to break the habit?

'Why do I keep doing this to myself?'

'Why didn't you just say "no"? What is wrong with me?!'

Have you started to resent others around you when you feel you get dumped on?

'They are real idiots, why can't they see that I don't have a way to do this?'

'I can't believe she just gave me that, but what else was there to do, I had to say ok.'

'I hate her!'

(✏) **Write down**

If you have answered 'yes' to any of the questions above, create this table for yourself. Firstly, identify your key areas of busy-busy-busy. Next write for each area all the gains of this activity. Separately, for each area write all the negatives, what you lose. Then consider: what do you conclude from this? Here's an example:

Situation	What do I gain?	What do I lose?	Conclusion
Work – taking on all these additional projects outside of my role	New colleagues Interest – current role is boring Career progress	Energy Ability to prioritise is weakened No time to see my friends at weekend Narky with family	Career important My own energy important Need to focus on projects that are genuinely interesting for me, so that my career direction is what I want! To do this new project, I need a plan of how to extricate myself from project a-b-c

Change

As a result of this process of thinking and writing, what would you like to change?

✔ **Commit**

What and who will help you shift from busy-busy-busy to a state where you feel energetic, motivated and at ease?

Consider the Top Enablers of resilience in Chapter 9.

Do It Yourself: How strong is your DIY tendency?

©The Resilience Engine 2019

✍ **Write down**

Circle your answers in the following chart.

If your answer varies according to different contexts, choose how you feel right now.

	Question	Score 1	Score 2	Score 3	Score 4
1.	How important is it to get things right?	Always important	Mostly important	Sometimes important, depends on situation	Not important
2.	How often do you ask for help to achieve the important things in your life?	Never	Sometimes	Often	Frequently

3.	How often do you feel people don't do things as well as they ought to?	Almost all the time	Often	Sometimes	Hardly ever
4.	How receptive are you to criticism?	Not receptive	Somewhat receptive	Often receptive	Always receptive
5.	How easy is it to delegate to others?	Impossible	Not easy but you do it	Quite easy depending on situation	Easy
6.	How bad do you feel when you've made a mistake?	Terrible	Bad	Quite bad	Not at all bad
7.	How many people do you trust to do things for you?	None	A handful	Quite a few	Loads!

Review
Reflect on your score and implications for yourself.

Scoring
Score 1: 10 points; Score 2: 6 points; Score 3: 3 points; Score 4: 0 points. Add up your scores for questions 1 to 7 to see what your total is.

0–21 Low DIY tendency
You are able to ask for help, and are comfortable trusting others to do important things for you. You are rarely defensive of your

projects. You are aware if you do feel defensive, and make the necessary adjustments to account for this.

If your score is at the higher end of this category, you do have scope to ask for help more often.

22–39 Warning! DIY tendency creep!

Your do-it-yourself tendency is getting in the way of your performance and wellbeing. It's worth considering the following questions:

○ What stops you from asking others for help?
○ If you are defensive of pet projects, what would help you build trust in others more?
○ If you find you are doing things perfectly but know you are into diminishing returns on your efforts, consider specifically what 'good' in this situation means.

40+ DIY as a badge of honour

Your DIY driver is holding you hostage and negatively affecting your performance and wellbeing. It is likely your wellbeing suffers first.

It is possible that this driver is deep-rooted. Where does it come from? Bringing awareness to this in you will help you understand. At some point in your life it was a good thing. Is it now?

⇨ Change

As a result of this process of this score, how can you help yourself ask for help more easily, more often?

✔ Commit

Commit to one situation where you can ask for help more. Give it a go.

Source: This tool is part of the Resilient Manager Toolkit service from The Resilience Engine. See http://www.resilienceengine. com/our-services/ for further information.

Stories of Resilience: Examples of Resilience Hooks in Action!

☺ The Resilience Lens

Have a look at this next scenario and see if you might be falling into the same situation.

Consider the options of the Resilient Way.

Consider what are you prepared to let go of, in order to shift to the Resilient Way.

Scenario 1

Your boss gives you something to do: *'That task is due by Monday morning'*. It's Friday morning and you are tied up all day, so the only way you can deliver this is by working at the weekend.

The Unresilient Way

Accepting this in the moment. Not asking for any flexibility. There are five sources of resilience drains here:

o Resenting and getting annoyed with yourself
o Not getting refreshed/perspective by taking quality time out at the weekend
o More dangerously, not being able to connect with meaning of home life by actually doing the work on Saturday afternoon, when the rest of the family is out

- o Most dangerously, fuelling your resentment towards your boss, and potentially with yourself
- o And lastly, creating a stuck pattern around this – not changing a thing having gone through all of this, so it's very likely to occur again.

The Resilient Way

As part of your resilience, you expect to notice, check in, learn, revisit and adapt throughout any situation. You will seek to feel ok in order to do this. This allows you to see different options. Here are some, starting with the most resilience:

Option 1

Seek help from others, including your boss, to accelerate each of the activities so you can still go home on Friday night without working at weekend. Plus explain to your boss how you would/ will prioritise the tasks. Offer the best solution that you can for completing the workload, with clear reasons, and verify with your boss that this solution is acceptable.

Speed of Reaction: Immediate
Quality of Reaction: High

Option 2

Having made the mistake of immediately accepting the deadline, going back during the day on Friday and revisiting the deadline with your boss, explaining capacity limitations. Part of option 1 still may be available.

Speed of Reaction: Later, but within work timeframe
Quality of Reaction: High

Option 3

Asking for verification from your boss about which tasks are highest priority for delivery. And waiting for response.

Speed of Reaction: Immediate
Quality of Reaction: Limited

Option 4

Having made the error of accepting the deadline, deciding not to do it at the weekend – wholly accepting this and letting go, trusting that you can sort it out on Monday – so you can enjoy the weekend.

On Monday, asking to be heard (and excused), recognising the difficulty for both of you, explaining why you felt it necessary to make those choices for your own health and wellbeing. Working through the implications with your boss.

Speed of Reaction: Much later
Quality of Reaction: Low at the time, but high later

☺ The Resilience Lens

Have a look at this next scenario and see if you might be falling into the same situation.

Consider the options of the Resilient Way.

Consider what are you prepared to let go of, in order to shift to the Resilient Way.

Scenario 2

You seek out challenges and ways of getting involved. People know you as being the person to sort things out, and you get a label for this. You end up with too much on your plate all the time, but you don't do anything to change it.

The Unresilient Way

Ploughing on. The resilience drains here are:

o   Energy
o   Loss of perspective means that other minor issues will appear huge
o   If long term, serious health consequences.

The Resilient Way

Those with the highest resilience probably have passed through this phase. This is definitely the domain of shifting to higher levels of resilience than Bounceback.

There is a need to fundamentally assess the criteria for what you get involved in – what is urgent, what is important, against what is genuinely meaningful for you.

In the short term, getting that space to think might be difficult. Seek help in the short term to reprioritise, to actually take some of the load off. When you start to see that some things on the to-do list are not important, go back and renegotiate the timeframe, or indeed drop the task. Say 'sorry, I am no longer able to do x-y-z'.

Then figure out how you are going to get quality thinking time and space, to reflect on your priorities.

Learn that saying 'no' means saying 'yes' to something else.

The Bottom Line

There is a big difference between the negative stress reaction and stressors. All stressors cause the same initial reaction, where adrenalin and cortisol secretion is triggered to cater for the mind/body needs in the initial stages of dealing with the stressor. This normal reaction is positive, and when the stressor settles, the reverse of the reaction occurs and the mind and body reset.

The negative stress reaction is when the reverse reaction in the body does not happen, and instead your system moves into normalising stress. Over time resistance collapses and the body becomes unwell.

This stress reaction is controlled initially by the brain and you have a choice in how you react. If your resilience is higher, you will have greater energy and perspective and will be able to give yourself options as to how you deal with any stressor. When your resilience is low, you will get hijacked because you do not have capacity to generate that flexible response.

The top three barriers to resilience that cause the negative stress reaction found in The Resilience Engine research are:

o   Weak or no boundaries
o   Overestimation of capacity
o   Do-it-yourself tendency.

Becoming aware of where you are hooked, accepting this, and then considering how you might loosen or shift the hook is part of the Resilient Way.

Chapter 8

Change and the Resilience Gap

'The issue for resilience is the gap between one's expectations versus capability.'

'It's definitely about being adaptive and flexible.'

Chapter Overview

This chapter expands on the strategic relationship between resilience and change. Organisational change is such a minefield of disasters and failures. If you account for resilience the odds of success will shoot up. Resilience is your capacity for change or your ability to adapt; it is the platform for all change.

In this chapter you are not going to read another set of do's and don'ts about change management. Instead, this chapter aims to express clearly why you need to think resilience when thinking about change.

The Resilience Scene

Change. There is so much written and talked about with regard to change, and more to the point, the failure of change. Most change programmes fail in organisations. McKinsey and Company show that 70% of all transformations fail.[80–84] It's not just McKinsey who say this. Harvard Business Review, Forbes, indeed almost all main management literature refer to the failure of change and change programmes:

Change is 'battle fatigue'.

Brent Gleeson in Forbes.com,
25 July 2017

Managers end up immersing themselves in an alphabet soup of initiatives… most change efforts exert a heavy toll.

Nitin Nohria and Michael Beer,
Harvard Business Review, May–June issue 2000

The content of change management is reasonably correct, but the managerial capacity to implement it has been woefully underdeveloped.

Ron Ashkenas, Harvard Business
Review, 16 April 2013

Change means responding to market place changes. It means responding to the new tasks within your role. It means responding to your team's changing needs. It means responding in your personal life:

o to your little kids in a different way, because whatever worked yesterday is not working right now!

o to an older relation over the way they can sometimes treat you, say in a patronising way. The pattern is long-grooved into both of your systems and tough to change. Yet you want to get rid of your reaction so you don't get annoyed each time you see them.

o to your changing health needs (sleep included!).

The list is endless. Every day you demand of yourself many, many adaptations, some little, some big.

However, change is only successful if there is sufficient resilience.

o When the demand for change exceeds the resilience potential, the resilience drain is too great. Resilience falls. Change fails or gets stuck.

o When the demand for change is equal to the resilience potential, the resilience equation is neutral – you manage day to day, but there is no surplus resilience available to take on any more change.

o When the demand for change is lower than the resilience potential, you're laughing. (As long as you keep that level of resilience potential going!)

The Resilience Engine Research Insight

Change is possible of course at the higher ends of resilience: the Whoosh upwards. At Breakthrough, change is easy. But change will fail if the 'ask' demands one level of resilience, whilst the actual capacity for change of the person/team/organisation which needs to enact the change is lower.

If there is a mismatch between the 'ask', the resilience demand versus the resilience potential, it gives rise to a Resilience 'Gap':

Change and the Resilience Gap

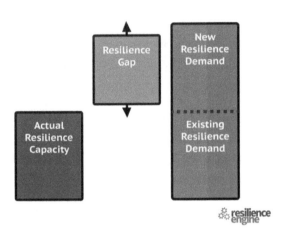

Take the following scenarios at different stages of The Resilience Dynamic® as examples:

Scenario 1: Bounceback, pretty high resilience but unstable

Consider the following conditions. Your resilience capacity at Bounceback is average, but it is under threat because you're juggling so much. This scenario is frequent amongst high performers. They love the thrill of the highs, but are tired of the highs and lows. This might be you. You know your resilience fluctuates. You can feel it, and so can others.

A new resilience demand comes along. On a good day, you might consider a bit of what you can do, and so it looks like you're making headway. Another day, it's simply in the too-difficult box. So nothing happens, even if you are pushing paper or decisions around.

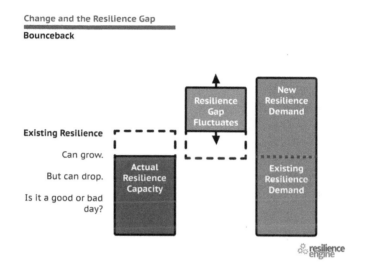

Change is definitely possible here, but unless there is more stability, there may not be enough capacity to successfully enact the change. The risk of mediocrity is high.

Scenario 2: Coping

This is when you're just managing. You have just enough capacity to enact what you need to do but there's no surplus. It's the zone where control is important and where you want to ensure things don't get out of control.

Here your resilience capacity can take on incremental change, as long as no significant learning is needed: improving that customer process, or improving a bit of workload management across your team, yes, that you can do. In your personal life you can also make some changes. Nothing significant like sorting out your relationship with your distant sibling whom you would really like to see more but don't manage to, and whom you feel further and further away from. Nothing like that, nothing major. But lots within the day to day is doable. Maybe with a bit of huff and puff, but it's ok.

On the other hand, a bigger demand comes along. Now that becomes a saga:

> *'How did it get to this?!'*
> *'What do people take me for?!'*
> *'How can they think it's ok?!'*

Or, if you have felt the stress reaction but your reaction is to capitulate, you've accepted somehow to try to make that change, but low and behold, everything slips and you aren't managing anymore.

Change and the Resilience Gap

Coping

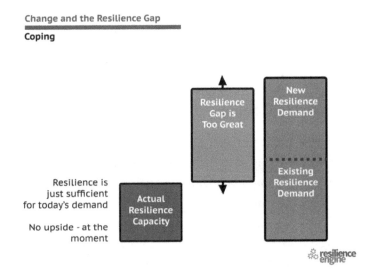

Only incremental, within-comfort-zone changes are possible at this level of resilience.

Scenario 3: Coping to Fragmentation, and Fragmentation itself

Not coping, either just slipping away from Coping or indeed at Fragmentation, are the states of resilience in the Resilience Dynamic® most dominated by negative stress. Your resilience capacity when not coping or at Fragmentation is low.

So many different people end up not coping at some stage or other in their lives:

o   Managers who aim high, want to do well, and who have the potential for higher resilience get themselves overloaded. They take so much on that their resilience drops terribly. If they don't shift something off their plate, they end up not coping.

o   Leaders who once were lauded for doing so well, riding on the crest of a wave, then suddenly are left behind because the new vanguard are in, and there is no room anymore for their skills. Lost, they can really lose their mojo, and end up not coping.

o   Those who are not coping in relationships, and because they have little support elsewhere, or cannot get away from that relationship, end up really feeling broken. Fragmentation.

o   Those who do well in life and are content but who have to manage a difficult health condition that limits what they can do. Coping at best, not coping at worst.

Change is a no-no in these resilience states.

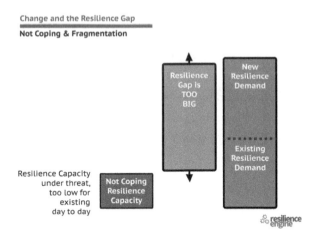

Even small, incremental changes here are really tough. Changes to routine, changes to the way people treat you, changes to your tasks, they will all be much more demanding than normal. Digging deep every day is the normal way to try to survive.

That is all rather bold. There is so much literature about change and change failures, it almost feels like you could suffer from change-analysis fatigue. Yet The Resilience Engine research data shows:

When you are not able to make change, think resilience. When people around you cannot adopt the change you are asking them to make, think resilience.

Applying the Resilient Way

Enough resilience?

©The Resilience Engine 2019

🔍 **Review**

Consider these questions:

o Have you ever been really keen to make a change for yourself but just not had the space to consider it properly or fully? So you keep hanging onto the dream of 'one day'?

o Have you tried to make a change via what seemed like a brilliant solution that in the end just didn't work? And you were so fed up with not getting the result that you gave up?

o Have you tried to enable change in others – your team at work, improve relationships within family members, at a local club – but despite them maybe even being obliged to make the change, they just don't succeed? Which leads to a whole load of inefficiency and potentially wasted effort?

Consider for each of your answers what your level of resilience was when managing or considering the change. Did your resilience match up to the resilience demand of the change?

Stories of Resilience

Sue and Fraser: A tale of the boss and the middle manager, neither of whom sees what's going

Introducing Fraser

Fraser is in finance. He's intellectually very smart, likes that about himself and others around him. He is single and leads in fact quite an easy life which he likes: reading, movies, friends. He doesn't have anything massively compelling outside of work to get stuck into. His work is therefore really important. It is compelling for many reasons: it occupies his active mind, plus he has debt he needs to pay off; Fraser really needs his job.

But he is drowning in workload. He was a rising star within the organisation and given a large team, but is now teetering. He just can't get his head around the lack of ability of others in his team to execute what he asks them. He ends up doing a lot himself.

Fraser is being asked to change how he manages his people, and particularly his relationships with them. His boss wants a happier workforce, and places the responsibility on Fraser to sort things.

Leading a big team demands changing his approach, but that seems out of reach for Fraser. Whilst he sees the deterioration of the relationships with his team, and wants and indeed commits to making changes, he can't really fathom out how on earth to address the issue. Instead he ploughs on hoping that something will give and he can make space to think about it.

Fraser's resilience level is just Coping, and that level going forward is under threat.

The Resilience Lens

Fraser is draining his Adaptive Capacity significantly. Whilst he has mental energy still, much of his work is dissatisfyingly dull. Working at weekends limits his time with his friends. Fraser's energy is not just flagging, it's draining out fast.

The energy drain is shunting him into being singularly minded and difficult. He holds an inflexible, often unreasonable perspective about his team and their capability. Interestingly he also has a do-it-yourself driver, believing that to ask for help is a failure.

◌ The Resilience Lens

In what ways do you identify with Fraser and his ways of doing things?

Introducing Sue

Sue, his boss, is suffering from a massive dent to her own personal confidence. Her resilience, normally high in both work and home, is lower than normal. It's not just a blip thing, it has been lower for a year or two, and she has almost forgotten what it's like to feel more at ease. Life is very demanding. And she finds herself questioning her own competence.

She has had to keep the Directorship going at the same time as supporting and managing the impact of her husband's unexpected illness. And that's the source of the resilience drain.

Sue's resilience is, on average, in the middle of Breakeven. With an abundant capability in terms of leadership – communication, strategy, capacity planning, asking for help – she has managed to cope during the really difficult periods, and indeed often led the organisation so adeptly through some really big changes during the past year. Her resilience oscillates between Coping and Bounceback. When in Bounceback, she deploys some of her admirable leadership skills more easily and consistently. When in Coping, she doesn't.

Sue, like Fraser, relies on her intellectual capability – her knowing – to understand what is happening around her. She also has the tendency to expect herself to work it out alone. She can ask for help on the strategic stuff; that's no problem! On personal stuff too. But Sue feels she ought to know, she needs to figure everything out herself.

She can see Fraser and his team in difficulty. She hears what Fraser says about the workload and his people. She sees him cracking. She feels a rising panic about the situation, and is wondering if Fraser is in fact near Breakdown. She has asked him to change, but has recently in her panic stepped into discussing structural changes that could help: workload reallocation across the team, anything really, to see if it helps. But Fraser isn't changing and her panic is greater. What should she do?

The Resilience Lens

Sue's resilience levels vary. When at the higher level, Sue can see the wood from the trees, and has more access to her own internal skills, and also finds it easier to ask for help from others. When her resilience levels are higher, she can accept more easily when she doesn't know something, and reaches out to get input and ideas from others.

When Sue's resilience is lower, she becomes super focussed and efficient. She can get through an enormous pile of work quickly. But her focus prevents her seeking other perspectives. And she also becomes fixed in her solutions. In this case, she can't see any other solution. Fraser needs to change, otherwise he will have to leave the organisation, she can't protect him much longer. But she also wants and indeed needs to keep him because she has no better alternative in the team.

Sue is stuck. She doesn't therefore shift anything in the situation and instead continues to interfere. She panics whilst doing this because she's fearful of Fraser genuinely breaking down. The whole thing in turn disrupts Fraser even more. He feels a diminishing of his authority and his autonomy. And that he finds unacceptable.

The Resilience Lens
In what ways do you identify with Sue and her assumptions about Fraser?

What happens in the situation?

Nothing changes until Fraser ends up being so cheesed off he leaves the organisation.

Sue is in part relieved, but now has to recruit someone else and deal with the impact of Fraser's departure. This demands more time and takes her away from an imperative which is to align around the strategy.

It's not a great result, for work outcomes or resilience outcomes. For both Sue and Fraser there is a further resilience drain, and this is really not good.

Was this result inevitable?

The Resilience Lens
Is there another way that this situation could have turned out? If so, what needed to change?

No learning was drawn from this situation; no learning was sought to change the situation. Neither Fraser nor Sue actually changed. And so neither did the situation. Change failed, despite both parties actually wanting change.

Why? Because their resilience levels were both too low for them to recognise their lack of capacity for change at the beginning. And instead of addressing resilience, they both stuck their head in the sand.

What might have changed?

The potential for Sue

Sue had the higher resilience levels and capability overall. She was the gateway for the change, but her own resilience needed a real boost for her to be able to see clearly how to help Fraser. She needed to accept her own needs first and foremost, and shift to address these. She also then needed to name and accept Fraser's level of capacity for change, and invite the conversation to get real around this as the first step.

Sue might have recognised Fraser's resilience more for what it was. He was oscillating between Coping and not coping. But he hadn't gone into Fragmentation: he remained pretty resourceful. He was not near Breakdown at all, and in fact could function well enough in all domains in his life. Sue needn't have panicked about how to handle a Breakdown; Fraser wasn't at that point.

The potential for Fraser

Fraser's biggest blocker was fear, and this stopped him from accepting the truth about him not coping. He didn't take responsibility for his own resilience; instead he shunted the blame for issues onto either his team, or indeed onto Sue as she started to try to help. Fraser saw this as interference rather than help.

The Bottom Line

This chapter has spelt out how resilience is at the heart of change; resilience needs to be at the heart of planning and managing all change. Where there is insufficient resilience in anyone, in any team, in any one system in fact, change is at risk.

Change needs investment in resilience, and an investment proportional to the actual resilience demand. It's not sufficient to tickle at resilience, to offer a sticky plaster. If the demand is big, then the investment equally needs to be big.

Part 3

How to Support and Develop Your Resilience

Chapter 9

Top Enablers of Resilience

'Self-awareness is key. It's taken a long time to understand that. It's the core of a personal state of resilience.'

'It's linked to energy; you need to maximise this. People who aren't resilient are too tired – hunger has worn off and success has taken its toll; people have lost their spark.'

'The pacing bit was the missing bit of the jigsaw… it's that understanding that you can do a great job but at the expense of what? 100% energy (leads to) 100% burnout.'

'We don't take time to stop and think and learn. Actually we keep going around this hamster wheel and we are delivering but actually there could be better ways of doing that.'

Chapter Overview

This chapter offers an overview of each of the Top Enablers so you can build the bedrock for your resilience.

Resilience is much more strategic than a set of tips, which is often what you will find on the internet if you search for how to develop resilience. It is much more strategic yet it is also simpler. There are some real fundamentals you need to develop for all of your resilience to flourish. That's what I concentrate on here, the Top Enablers. They are the platform for your resilience.

The Resilience Scene

There is a lot of noise about resilience and wellbeing. Having been in the field since 2007 when it wasn't talked about very much at all, it's now all the rage. And in that noise, it's difficult to resist jumping to what is offered as the silver bullet, or the 'Top 5 resilience boosters' or the top 10, 25, 64, or even the 'one'.

> The NHS offers six ways.
> MIND offers four overarching themes in which there are twenty specific tips.
> The International Stress Management Association offers a series of ideas based on different themes, often in bundles of ten tips.
> ... and many more!

These are all reputable organisations, and all are aiming to offer something genuine, real, actionable. Often these tips are offering something specific but end up being too generic; they are meant for general consumption and may not match your resilience levels. It's similar to Growth versus Fixed Mindsets. As Carol Dweck laments, you don't need

> a list of unconnected pointers like 'Take more risks!' or 'Believe in yourself.'[22]

Whilst The Resilience Engine research shows that there are three Top Enablers of resilience, plus a fourth from Bounceback upwards, it's up to you how to make these come alive in your work and life.

These are just the first steps towards resilience; they are the platform from which your resilience can grow. They give you the fundamentals, but they are not everything. Thereafter there are a set of attitudes and beliefs involved. These include being able to hold your own power whilst remaining humble; forgiveness; being able to balance your drive for independence and dependence. There are skills involved, associated often with management and leadership including prioritisation; horizon scanning; seeking different perspectives and voices; influencing; alignment of capacity according to demand. These are all part of your Resilience Engine®, The Resilience Engine's model of how to build resilience.

To start off with, however, your resilience platform relies on the Top Enablers of resilience. Concentrating initially on these gives you such a fantastic solid base for everything else. They will flush out the big stuff, and they are very easy to put in place.

The Resilience Fundamentals

When you pare the lists offered around resilience and wellbeing back to the bare bones, you uncover the heart of resilience. The fundamentals of resilience are not simplistic but they are simple and deep. The Resilience Engine research shows three Top Enablers of resilience, and a fourth that kicks in at very specific levels of resilience. Embracing these as part of your day to day will revolutionise your performance and wellbeing.

Further, they are not a list. They are interdependent – all enablers are needed and work together as part of the Resilient Way.

The top three enablers are:

o   Being present. Being able to be present right here, right now.

This is the ability to just 'be'. It enables you to be calm and feel grounded. In skill terms, it enables you to notice more, to widen your perspective, to listen to yourself and to others, and therefore really 'see' the resilience data that is available

201

to you. It also allows you to connect with your vision of what you want in any situation.

o   Energy. Maximising your energy – all elements of this.

This is crucial. As I've said earlier, energy and resilience follow the same ups and downs. Investing in your energy isn't all of your resilience, but gosh, it's a real fast-track to boosting it!

o   Learning – how you learn, not just what you learn.

This is available to you once you're right in the middle of Breakeven. It's a kind of tipping point in the Resilience Dynamic® that signals that a small surplus of capacity for learning has been made available. You have time not just to do-do-do, but to do-think-do-think. The real core to shifting way out to the higher levels of resilience resides in this core ability, to learn well.

Then there is a fourth enabler that kicks in from Bounceback upwards:

o   Purpose.

This is about making the meaning in your life come alive day to day. It's more than goals, it's about enacting the things you really care about, that you 'bond'[13] to.

> Bonding to goals provides the determination and resilience to overcome obstacles and achieve results. The very act of bonding to a goal brings energy to the pursuit.[13]

Purpose fosters the specific goals you have for yourself and your life, and these in turn, provide the direction of travel across your work and life. Purpose is only worth getting into if you are either at Bounceback upwards, or in fact at the lowest level of resilience, Breakdown. By (re)connecting to your purpose, you re-galvanise energy towards the important stuff of life that really matters.

Embedding these enablers as part of your day-to-day habits will enable transformational change. Embracing these, and learning to eliminate the barriers to resilience, is the path towards feeling at ease.

How the Resilience Enablers Work

Top Enabler 1: Being present

This gives an ability to rest, to give the body and mind a chance to recuperate, breathe and restock. It helps resettle any stress response that has been happening, that amygdala hijack referred to in Chapter 7. Research in 2019 from Oxford and Exeter Universities[85] shows *'being kind to oneself switches off the threat response and puts the body in a state of safety and relaxation that is important for regeneration and healing'.*

Being present encourages you to open up and notice first, then accept, your own emotions. It helps you notice fully and accept the responses of others. As a result, you are better able to identify, experience and process these emotions. This widens your perspective on yourself and on other people, plus on other matters such as the truth behind business issues and challenges.

Being present relies on your ability to be both compassionate and curious. Compassion for yourself: to forgive yourself for what you have done or have felt, or are feeling and thinking. Curious: to seek to understand more, to seek to discover more.

Seeing truthfully what is really going on is absolutely fundamental to resilience. You need the ability to see the truth of any situation (even if there are several truths), and to generate different options to address that situation according to different outcomes.

Look at the table below on the difference between Doing versus Being. The Resilient Way is to do both easily.

Doing	Being
Automatic pilot	Conscious choice
Analysing	Sensing
Striving	Accepting
Seeing thoughts as truth	Thoughts as mental events
Avoiding	Approaching
Mental time travel	Staying in the present
Outputting/Deleting	Inputting/Nourishing

Source: ©Table copyright of The Resilience Engine.

Q **Review**

How often do you find yourself on the left-hand side?
How often do you find yourself on the right-hand side?

Whilst both are necessary for resilience (indeed you must be able to 'do' in order to learn and not be in analysis-paralysis mode), being present bears a stronger influence on your resilience because of the ongoing perspective it offers.

Top Enabler 2: Energy

The Resilience Engine research shows that energy and resilience are directly correlated. This applies to individuals, but also to teams and in fact whole organisations. If you plot one on a graph across time, the shape of the other will follow the same line on the graph.

The Resilient Way is to maximise your energy. A question to hold every day is **'How can I maximise my energy today?'** There are several sources of energy:

Your physical energy

Contributors include your sleep, the amount and intensity of exercise you do, health conditions you may have, your weight, and factors that drive your physical stamina such as muscle definition, your cardiovascular function, etc.

What does physical energy do for you? You get a boost of endorphins, the natural hormones that get released when you are doing something that requires a burst of energy. They are the ones that make you move. It's the endorphin release that contributes to feeling good, or even euphoric, commonly known as the 'runner's high'.[86] You boost your cardiovascular system, which increases your endurance. That in turn means you have more energy in the tank, and if you're not using it all up, you have a bit of surplus left.

Your mental energy

It's all about choosing what you do when, and ensuring there is enough in the tank left for the important stuff.

Research published in *Scientific American*[87] shows that you have a limited amount of mental energy to spend each day. Once that resource is depleted your decision making and productivity decline rapidly. That means your capacity for change has diminished. It means that instead of being able to proact, you will shift to react more.

This is why it is a good idea to tackle the most important projects first when your mind is fresh regardless of how time-consuming those projects may seem. By the end of the day, your mental energy is waning and it will be harder to focus and critically think. *'Our brains are configured to make a certain number of decisions per day and once we reach that limit, we can't make any more, regardless of how important they are,'* explains Daniel J. Levitin in his book *The Organized Mind: Thinking Straight in the Age of Information Overload.*[88]

Your emotional energy

The research on the links between performance and feeling positive, happy and confident is comprehensive. [83,84,89–94] Invest in what gives you joy! The alternative, not being able to express your emotions, or worse, somehow stifling them so they don't show up to anyone else, that is the stuff of resentment and significant energy drain.

Your spiritual energy

Put simply, it's what you get inspired by. This unlocks new possibilities. *'Inspiration awakens us to new possibilities by allowing us to transcend our ordinary experiences and limitations. Inspiration propels a person from apathy to possibility, and transforms the way we perceive our own capabilities.'* [95–98] Inspiration involves both being inspired by something and acting on that inspiration.

Top Enabler 3: Learning

To be resilient means adapting successfully to change. Adaptability doesn't happen without learning. And the learning is not just about what you learn, but how you learn it.

For resilience, there is continuous learning about emotions and the sources of emotions in yourself and in others. There is continuous adjustment to account for new circumstances. This is true as much for individuals as it is for teams, as it is for the whole organisation.

🔍 Review

What do you need to learn about for your resilience's sake?

o How to 'be' more?
o How to maximise your energy?
o How to learn better?

You have to unlearn the stuff that doesn't help anymore. What do you need to unlearn for your resilience's sake?

o How to let go of control?

o How to be less compliant and stop saying 'yes' all the time?

o How not to be so tough, but instead to be softer?

Past performance doesn't necessarily make for a happy future – anyone can be caught in traps from the past. Liisa Valikangas[99] defined organisational resilience in 2010 as a capacity to undergo deep change without or prior to a crisis. In 2010 Valikangas listed the issue of 'Fallen Eagles': expired rules that are no longer fit for purpose. They make scary reading since so many of them are practised still today:

o *Planning is sufficient preparation for the future.* What about unpredictable events?

o *Good strategy is key to success.* Most organisations linger in transition between the old strategy that doesn't work and the new one which is yet to be fully implemented.

o *People behave rationally.* Example: we easily rush to imitate, even if what we copy is rubbish!

o *Copying best practices cannot be argued against.* Copying to create something new isn't possible when the old processes and habits still reside inside.

o *It is best to wait until change is absolutely necessary to save cost.* I think this one is self-evident!

o *The art of management is about executing against pre-established goals and optimising performance.* We are seeing the drive for innovation as new means of creating value, not just being even more efficient.

And finally, you need to pay attention to how you learn, and if needed, improve on that.

 Review

How do you need to learn for your resilience's sake?

- Less doing, more reflecting?
- Less analysing, just decide and then move on?
- More looking at the real truth of the situation, 'the resilience data', and therefore seeing more clearly what is going on and the options you may have?

If you don't learn, you will continue to do the same things, and get the same results. If you are creating results that are mediocre, you'll get mediocrity. If you are creating results that are failing, you'll get failure. If you create poor relationships for yourself, without learning, you will continue to do the same with any new ones.

The Resilient Way is to enable enough capacity to learn as you go. Those operating in Breakthrough embrace learning. They are not caught up by a rule-book. They are not scared to give themselves time to sense what they are experiencing and change their plans accordingly. At the same time, they can notice what's going on and stand firm in their planned path. Both are valid, and the options are explicitly examined and re-decided on an ongoing basis. Resilient people interrupt old patterns and old habits where these don't serve their purpose any longer.

Emergent learning relies on being present to what is around us right now. If you cannot learn to 'be' in the moment, learning in the moment is not possible. If you cannot sense what is going on inside you, outside you, in others, your ability to respond to the actual situation will be limited. If you override your senses and ignore what's going on, you are building trouble. If you are overriding the signals of stress, of exhaustion or ill health, you are on your way to Fragmentation.

Resilience means being with all your previous past experiences, and taking that into the moment right now, and as such leading yourself towards a different future. It's what Otto Scharmer from MIT in his U Process might describe as 'connecting with our emergent future'.[100]

Top Enabler 4: Purpose

Purpose is the fourth fundamental enabler of resilience, but that shows up in very specific places in the Resilience Dynamic®. To recap, purpose is important from Bounceback upwards; purpose is really the thing that distinguishes those who are stuck in Coping from those who are on the Whoosh, who feel both satisfied and at ease in their life. Purpose also is significant at Breakdown, once the person has had enough rest, energy and help.

Your purpose is likely to include the aspects of your job or career that you love. It will include the people and activities outside of work. You might play a sport and love being part of that team. You might be a parent and put tremendous effort into, and derive tremendous pride and love from, parenting well. You might be involved in enabling a new societal way of tackling the environment, starting off with your own community. Your purpose is what Simon Sinek calls your 'why',[101] or what George Kohlrieser calls part of your 'secure bases'. [5,13]

Purpose is about being inspired. As Simon Sinek says,

if your actions inspire others to dream more, learn more, do more and become more, you are a leader... if you hire

people just because they can do a job, they'll work for your
money.[102]

But it's more than being inspired – things that inspire you may include things **outside** of your purpose; they give you a lift, they energise you – but they may not be **your** thing. What's inspiring about these is that they inspire you to become inspired for yourself!

You need to search for what is meaningful to you. You may have a purpose in work, you may have a purpose in your sport, you may have a purpose in your family life. All are valid. The meaning must be yours, not someone else's. The Resilient Way isn't just to have a purpose in theory, but to find a way of making that purpose come alive in your work and life. Your purpose is all about enactment. It's about connecting up what is meaningful to your actions in your life.

When life sways off course from your purpose or if you feel that the goals you have in the end drain you, it can be hard to feel like you're on the right path. That's when purpose really kicks in. It's beyond specific goals – it's like a guiding light ahead. Steve Jobs said in his Stanford speech in 2005[103] to graduating students:

Believing that the dots will connect down the road will give
you the confidence to follow your heart.

In this speech he mentions trusting your gut, destiny and life and how that all leads you towards something. Purpose is about connecting the dots.

Purpose is pretty much listed in every place you find resilience. Yet it's not necessarily the thing to work on. It depends on your resilience level.

The relevancy of purpose versus resilience level

Purpose is really relevant for those who wish to shift to beyond Bounceback. Purpose is also relevant to those who have suffered a Breakdown. So it's straightforwardly relevant at almost the two opposite ends of The Resilience Dynamic®.

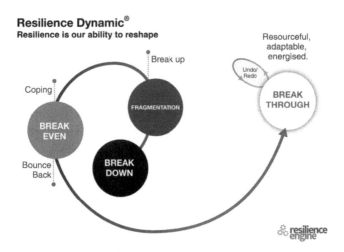

Resilience Dynamic®
Resilience is our ability to reshape

Breakdown

The cause of Breakdown is often that someone has been trying to live in a particular way that is incompatible with who they really are. They have experienced deep incoherence. This can happen because they haven't connected to their own sense of meaning in life. Instead they have been living by some other meaning, maybe someone else's meaning, or some kind of dreamt-up meaning that they thought was good for them. And it didn't work. It means they end up breaking.

As part of the process of understanding and shifting from Breakdown, once the person is more stable and is more well, purpose comes into play again. First of all it's about letting go of any old meaningless purpose that was part of the cause of the Breakdown in the first place. Then the work changes to uncovering, discovering and connecting with their true purpose.

Purpose work here is fabulous; it's uplifting and inspiring. And it can be tough, because someone in Breakdown will have some parts of themselves hidden. There is guilt, shame and fear, and these all block that possibility of creation of real meaning. Yet because the Breakdown is so clear to the person and to others, with the help of others, someone coming out of Breakdown may generate enough capacity for purpose creation.

Beyond Bounceback

At the other end of the Resilience Dynamic®, from Bounceback upwards, purpose, supporting by learning, is the big daddy of resilience. This is certainly true for individuals, and from the recent Resilience Engine research, we think also for teams and organisations.

Why purpose matters at these resilience levels

Consider these reasons:

Purpose shifts your thinking from the internal to external. That means you're less hijacked by negative self-talk.

Purpose makes you less self-centred. You are part of something bigger, outside of you, and so you focus less on your own stuff. Your own stuff in fact seems less difficult or less important as a result.

Purpose is closely linked to 'flow' – the state of intense absorption in which you forget your surroundings and yourself. If you have a strong sense of purpose, you're likely to experience flow more frequently. Mihaly Csikszentmihalyi[2] has shown that flow is a powerful source of wellbeing and happiness.

Purpose can also enhance self-esteem. If there is a sense of success as you work for your purpose, you feel a sense of achievement in each step.

Finally, purpose is closely related to hope. Hope is linked also to wellbeing. This is very evident with patients suffering from serious long-term illness: a high level of hope brings both an increased ability to cope, and a greater chance of recovery.[104]

Where connecting to purpose is not possible

If you are in chronic Coping, or indeed chronic Fragmentation, connecting with the idea of purpose in the first place may seem a joke: 'I've not got time for that, that's for someone else!' Indeed, part of the reason you're in chronic Coping or Fragmentation is probably related to an unclear purpose, or at least one that is very disconnected from your reality day to day.

To uncover, to explore and to draw not just hope but an ability to live your purpose means working at it. It means de-layering any false notions you have of yourself, seeing yourself fully without any smokescreen. To do that work takes a whole lot of mental and emotional energy. But at chronic Coping or

Fragmentation, you just don't have that energy. Only once your resilience has shifted to a higher level and is stable, can you really get to work on what your purpose is.

So don't try. Instead work on the enablers of being present and energy; these are practical enablers that you can do something about.

If you're a coach or manager, and working with someone in this particular situation, then really take this research insight into account. There is no point in asking a member of your team in work, who hasn't been Coping for a long time, to consider what purpose they have. They may find it patronising, and may react accordingly: defensively, even aggressively. Or they may try to please you and seem to join in the discussions on purpose. You may be duped into thinking they are sorted, they are on their way, they are reconnected. But in truth, they have agreed with you so that the overwhelm caused by your focus on them is removed.

Many people will dream whilst in this situation. Daydreaming of a better time is a Coping mechanism. It is great, it is helpful! But it's not the same as purpose. Purpose is when you can take what is meaningful to you, and do something about it for real.

Coping but still able to connect with purpose

If you have had high resilience and for some reason find yourself in a Coping situation, say for health reasons, or a difficult family situation, or because of a huge project at work that is draining all your energy, purpose work is possible. In these situations, connecting with your purpose will give you energy; a spiritual energy that brings possibility and hope. And that in turn can widen perspective, and your creative juices start to flow more. Options and solutions tumble forth.

As Steve Jobs said, going forward in life, you can't predict everything or set up all the dots in advance. You've got to do the dance of the dots instead – as they unfold and bump into you. But your navigation through your work and life, your choices of what you do and how you are, can be ignited by your purpose, by what's meaningful for you.

 Review

What do your dots look like?
Are they connecting to a purpose that is meaningful for you?

Stories of Resilience

Emma

Emma has a good life. She has a great job in the NHS as Nursing Director. She is doing something she loves and believes in. It's too busy but she can handle it, whilst in her home life she has a lovely and loving husband and her kids are great.

That's at least how it should be.

Emma is actually over-working, covering in another NHS Trust for a maternity leave absence, and recovering from the aftermath of a bullying case in her own division. Staff still feel unsettled. She as Director has had to deal with a lot of unpleasant behaviour. She could do with things just turning the corner.

Emma is a driver of things in life. She likes organising things, and for things to be organised. She likes tidiness, clarity, methodical people, things being complete. Whilst she admires and loves the idea of being more free, for her, she is best with a steady, quality way of handling things. All ok in work, but these needs spill right out into family life when she's tired.

216

Her husband, whom she loves, is a journalist. He is often out and about, often under massive pressure to get work in on time. And he is messy. In lots of ways, from his desk in his office, through to how he throws the dirty laundry on the bedroom floor and rushes out in the morning. He's brilliant, he's fun, he's creative and in Emma's mind, he is 'free'. But he is downright messy.

Emma doesn't like this but has learnt that her needs in terms of tidiness around the house are mostly met by her. So she sorts the washing herself, or when things get a bit haywire, she will sit down and chat with the family about her needs, and everything in the house slightly readjusts to something she can deal with. Emma thinks this is all pretty reasonable and certainly within the limits of what she can handle.

Except when she's massively under pressure. In this state, Emma vociferously detests the mess. And instead of asking for what she needs, she complains, undermines anyone who is messy, or gets angry. Since she believes that anger is wrong (at least to show it is!), she absorbs as best she can all these feelings. Over time these feelings can build inside, causing resentment. And that leads to a hardness in Emma that she has also come to really dislike.

The rotten cycle has affected her joy at home, and she wants to change.

The Resilience Lens

Emma is both capable and has a resilience level hovering around Bounceback. Within her home territory of nursing it's higher.

So Emma knows what it feels like to be at a higher level of resilience; she understands what it's like to be adaptable, flexible – and the benefits that this brings. She can adapt herself according

217

to the needs of different situations, and can shift her own needs at home to establish a harmonious environment for everyone.

Emma's resilience has been under a great deal of pressure for a prolonged period. Her energies are low, her sleep is affected, and she has started to beat herself up for her reactions to things. She has shifted from proactive to reactive, and it is beginning to be a habit. Emma's resilience levels now are at best Coping. But she carries still the resources from a higher level, and so whilst Coping, she can perform relatively well, it just takes a lot more out of her than it used to.

Emma needs to rest more. It's quite basic. She needs to rest, she needs to get joy, she needs to step away from other people needing her so much and just 'be'. Being present is a key enabler of resilience, and enables both calm and wellness, but also perspective. It's that perspective that Emma sorely needs. Others around Emma might also offer that to her – her colleagues at work, and her family at home.

The biggest thing for Emma is to accept that it's ok to need what she needs, ie for things to be calm and tidy at home, to feel restful. If Emma recognises this as a resilience issue it will help her change her approach.

She can learn to accept that during this period her resilience is low and therefore she doesn't have capacity for the change to accommodate the messiness of her husband and her family. Instead of dealing with the output from the issue of messiness, Emma needs to invest in feeling rested, joyful and to get perspective.

This would help her rekindle the capacity to re-adopt her normal routines, without resentfulness. She would feel better!

☺ The Resilience Lens

What resonated for you in Emma's story?

Do you also have one area of your life that has got demanding but because of the cultural norms, you feel inhibited in your ability to manage it well, and instead it spills over into other parts of your life?

Are there people or situations that you are starting to resent but wish you didn't?

Which of the Top Enablers do you need most in order to prevent these kinds of situations arising?

The Bottom Line

The fundamentals of resilience rely on your getting a platform for it to build on. This platform can be considered a layering-up of the following Top Enablers of resilience:

Being present
Energy in all its forms
Learning, particularly how to learn better
And finally purpose for Bounceback levels and above, plus coming out of Breakdown.

This chapter explains why these are the fundamentals; Chapter 10 gives you the tools to develop each of these.

Chapter 10

What to Do for Each Resilience Level

'Focussing on priorities, this builds resilience.'

'I can recall great moments and bring them to the present.'

'You have to look after yourself on behalf of the team so no-one else has to carry you. You can't be a prima donna.'

'You have to be open to being counter-intuitive.'

Chapter Overview

This chapter will take all of the ideas in the book and help you create your own Resilient Way. The chapter is set out in two main sections:

o   The first is a synopsis of the Resilient Way for each resilience level of the Resilience Dynamic®.

o   The second is a deeper 'How to' section on the Top Enablers of resilience: being present, energy, learning and purpose.

Section 1: Synopsis of the Resilient Way for Each Resilience Level on the Resilience Dynamic®

Resilience level		Whoosh/Breakthrough
Resilience aims & fast track		Alignment of life towards purpose Keep learning
The Resilient Way		
Being		Slow down often
Energy	Physical	Flex your exercise according to how you really feel
	Emotional	Invest in one or two relationships that you have let go of
	Mental	Practise mind-wandering and see how creative you can get
	Spiritual	Practise self-compassion
Learning		Still got stuff to learn in current context? Got a few triggers/hooks? Look at the resilience data of the situation Or a bit stagnant? Step outside of your comfort zone. Do something zany!
Purpose		Keep stretching goals towards your purpose Is your purpose shifting?

Resilience level		Bounceback
Resilience aims & fast track		Stabilise at higher levels of energy. What do you have to learn in order to stabilise your energy? Then and only then rediscover and connect more coherently with purpose. How can you align more of what you do to things that are meaningful for you?
The Resilient Way		
Being		S-l-o-w down When you eat When you walk When you talk S-l-o-w down
Energy	Physical	Get exercise into your routine
	Emotional	Say 'no' to something. Start with what's simple
	Mental	Make thinking time. Make it unnegotiable
	Spiritual	Connect with something you love, or used to love, doing
Learning		Face up to what you need to learn about yourself that is driving the ups and downs
Purpose		Take some time to map out what you are doing that is meaningful and what you are doing that isn't Notice from previous stories, events etc. what has given you the most satisfaction in your life

Resilience level		Stuck in the middle of Breakeven
Resilience aims & fast track		To unlock any stuckness. What do you need to accept about yourself and how you are creating the conditions for stuckness? To shift to Bounceback
The Resilient Way		
Being		Consider what you have to accept about your work and life How much of it is you creating the conditions for being stuck? How can you do this truthfully?
Energy	Physical	Change something – either create a routine or change it
	Emotional	Change something – step outside of the ordinary so you feel something full on
	Mental	Imagine
	Spiritual	Connect with something you love, or used to love, doing
Learning		Face up to what you need to learn about yourself that creates stuckness
Purpose		Imagine and wonder Hang out with people that inspire you

Resilience level		Coping
Resilience aims & fast track		To stabilise Coping Get more energy. Invest in sleep/have a laugh/ take time to breathe and just switch off
The Resilient Way		
Being		Reclaim/create some me-time. Each day if you can. Even 10 minutes will help Examples: Take a slightly longer shower in the morning Walking slowly
Energy	Physical	Get some exercise that raises your heart rate a bit. Even walking fast or going up the stairs at work
	Emotional	Laugh! Examples: Be with someone who you like laughing with Watch a funny film
	Mental	Each day, think of something to be thankful for. They can be very, very simple things Examples: I feel the sun on my face I get to see my kids today I have enough food on my plate
	Spiritual	Pat yourself on the back for Coping. It's brilliant·that you are
Learning		N/A
Purpose		N/A

Resilience level		Fragmentation
Resilience aims & fast track		To cope
		Step away from the sources of stress as much and as often as possible
		Accept that you're stressed
		Rest
		Be with someone who cares
		Move gently
The Resilient Way		
Being		When you're feeling overwhelmed, it's useful to take a moment. For you and you only
		You are not responsible for anything in that moment
		You don't need to be anything in that moment
		Just be
Energy	Physical	When you are feeling tired, allow yourself some recovery time
		Examples:
		When you arrive back in from work, sit down and close your eyes for 10 minutes
		After a difficult meeting, take 5 minutes and just sit at your desk, do nothing
	Emotional	Identify one of the things that is stressing you – the stressor
		For one day or part of a day, avoid that stressor
		If it's a continual worry, consider right here, right now, at this very moment, what your best influence can be on that. Often it's to resource yourself more, and that way you'll have more energy and perspective on the matter. This in turn will lead to options for shifting the stressor
	Mental	Ask at work, or at home, if you can reduce the load by stopping some of the tasks you have on your plate
	Spiritual	Be gentle on yourself
Learning		N/A
Purpose		N/A

Resilience level		Breakdown
Resilience aims & fast track		Stop and rest
		Acceptance
		Be with someone who cares
		Seek professional help
The Resilient Way		
Being		Take some time for you and you only
		You are not responsible for anything in that moment
		You don't need to be anything in that moment
		Just be
Energy	Physical	**Focus on sleep**
		Get fresh air
		Move gently
		Stick to the same times each day
		Check that your room is cool, doesn't have too much light, isn't next to too much noise, and that there is good ventilation
		Make sure you have a comfortable mattress and pillow
	Emotional	Get a hug from someone who cares for you
	Mental	Seek out something you love, or have loved Examples: nature, kids doing or saying funny things, listening to music, being in silence
	Spiritual	Be proud of one thing you do in the day. Like getting up, putting on lipstick, or calling someone
		Celebrate the simple things you are managing to do
Learning		N/A
Purpose		N/A

Section 2: Applying the Resilient Way Enablers in More Detail

How to: Be present

©The Resilience Engine 2019

 **Write down**

How are you at being?

Just being.

Not racing to do-do-do, just be?

What about as you read this book? If your mind is elsewhere you're not right here, right now.

✔ **Commit**

Ensure that you take time and space to yourself each and every day. Even a little bit.

What does this entail for you?

🔍 **Review**

Which of these is attractive?

- o   Yoga
- o   Breathing, focussing on the breath each day to enjoy and really feel it
- o   5 or 10 minutes of silence
- o   Having a quiet cup of coffee with the papers
- o   Listening to music
- o   Dozing
- o   Crafting
- o   Playing an instrument
- o   Walking the dog

There is no one way. The Resilient Way is to work this out for yourself, so that you can be here, right here, right now.

✍ Change

Here are some being present tips:

○ **Ensure that you breathe well.**

This is one of the core skills of being present. Noticing your breathing, changing your breathing as you would wish, allowing the breath to fill you up. It centres you.

One minute breathing

This is about counting how many breaths you take in a minute. There is no need to do anything different to your breathing, just allow the breath to come as it comes.

Have a timer nearby. When you're ready, start the timer and count how many breaths you take in that minute.

Everyone will have a different number. Mine is five, for example, whereas other people might reach a number closer to 20. No matter. It's your count that's important.

You can now use that at anytime, anywhere. Imagine:

You are racing to a meeting, late. You enter, feeling frazzled. The meeting has started, you take your place, but your mind is racing all over the place. Count your number of breaths in a minute. Notice that you will have calmed your mind, your body and you will be able to listen and contribute better.

Someone has said something that enrages you. Your instinct is to blow! But you know it could make things worse. Instead, count your number of breaths in a minute. Give you, and the other person, a chance to get perspective on the situation.

You have tonnes to do all day, but it's your evening appointment that really matters to you. You are distracted by excitement all day, but it's affecting everyone else around you and they are getting annoyed that you aren't listening properly. Count your number of breaths in a minute. It will help you notice directly what is going on, with yourself and with others. You might notice also that your relationship with your colleagues matters, as well as your evening appointment. And having the two together is quite possible, so you can settle a little more.

o **Allow yourself off the hook when you're tired and can't focus.**

You have a choice:

Beat yourself up about not being able to do x-y-z.

Trudge on.

Or allow a little light of 'being present' to help you shift a little. It makes a huge difference. Free-wheel for a bit first – then see what difference that can make.

o **Look for beauty in life.**

In nature, in people laughing and smiling, in kids, when you see people caring for one another. Connect with joy and beauty; it's so lovely. Even when you're not coping, this is available to you. Go out and let the beauty that is around you come into you. It will help you 'be'. Floods of tears may come, and they will help you release whatever you are holding. Make sure someone is there to give you a hug afterwards!

o **Be thankful.**

This is another idea that has become a bit wishy washy. But how can it be over-used?! It's just so wise. When you realise what you have, you want for less.

How to: Energy

This is a deceptively simple idea. How can you get more energy? How can you stop the energy drain? It sounds too obvious. The experience of The Resilience Engine is that it's difficult to actually know this in reality. People think that thing, or so-and-so, will give them energy, but it doesn't turn out that way. It depends.

Going out on a Friday with friends normally is brilliant, you love it, good chat, good vibes. But this week you are tired, you haven't slept so well and you had meant to finish clearing up that room in your house that you started at the weekend, and if you go out on Friday late, you'll be knackered and not do it until Sunday, and that won't be enough time to finish it, so you'll be annoyed, and… and… And you could get so annoyed at the situation, it all feels jammed. And you could get further annoyed at yourself for allowing this to happen. You can't stand it when you feel like this!!!!

You could just let yourself off the hook and not go out on Friday.

Managing your energy might mean saying 'no' to quite a lot of people and to things you had planned. Managing your energy means saying 'yes' to some specific things you know are good for you. Like sleeping better, having a free weekend so that you can be with the family, getting that time for the gym, or just calling up an old mate and having a really good natter. Once you get it into your head that you know you feel better doing the things that are good for your energy, you'll want to do them more and more.

To start, however, you've got to know what having energy feels like. The Resilience Engine uses an energy mapping tool so you can see for yourself what contributes to your energy going up and down. Have a go.

The Resilience Engine energy mapping tool

©The Resilience Engine 2019

(✏) **Write down**

On the following graph, plot your overall energy across time. The period of time to plot against will depend on the relevance to your energy of the different contexts in which you operate:

o Are you thinking of your real day to day? Map across the last 7 days.

o If you are seeking to understand how your resilience has been across a longer period and using energy as a proxy, choose the period most significant for you. It may be the last 3–6 months, or it could be the last year, or indeed the last 18 months to 2 years.

🔍 Review

Once you're done, either chat it through with a friend or coach, or consider by yourself.

o   What contributes to the up parts?
o   What contributes to the down parts?
o   And is the overall level where I would like it to be?

What do you discover in this process?

You might experience your energy in different ways.

You know when you have it:
o   You feel groovy.

o   You are bouncy.

o   You feel and indeed are creative.

o   You can focus easily.

You know when you don't have it:
o   You know if you're dragging yourself around.

o   You know that sense of your head being jammed.

o   You know when you just can't handle another minor argument at home but don't have the energy to intervene.

o   You keep yawning.

o   You sleep heavily but when you wake up, you're still not refreshed.

And then there are the in-between times when it's not so clear what your energy is doing!

o   You might have high mental energy but be physically tired.

o   You know when you're too tired to talk with others but might be able to focus on writing a paper.

o   You might be full of tension, a form of energy that is consuming you.

o   You might feel uplifted spiritually but not have the physical or mental energy to enact what has inspired you.

You can decide in many situations to override what you actually need and keep going. If you keep doing that again and again of course, things will go awry. In the short term, it's just that day's performance at risk. Like at the end of the day when critical decisions have to be made but you're tired and can't see the wood from the trees but you decide something anyway. Or when you are due to meet an important person and you come over as just not that interested. If you are overriding your energy and pushing yourself to continue, your decisions will be poorer, your relationships put at risk.

One of the most surprising things for those of us working in resilience is that high-potential resilience people, often leaders, destroy all that good resilience by draining their energy by taking on too much. There is a tendency to keep going because they think they have endless energy. Result? A resilience reduction. If lucky they will move to Bounceback or Coping, but they could end up in burnout,[105] a special form of Fragmentation. The executive draining their energy like this so much that they fall over is entirely shocked that they couldn't keep it up.

Energy counts a lot in performance.

All the world of efficiency can help you reduce unnecessary-to-do's. If you are left, however, with a whole lot of must-do's, what do you do? You have to input something additional. That can be counter-cultural; there is a drive for efficiency, rather than taking space to top up your energies.

🔍 Review

Look at the Energy Equation below. Which category does your overall energy fall into?

The Energy Equation	Result
Energy Inputs < Energy Outputs	Depletion
Energy Inputs = Energy Outputs	Coping
Energy Inputs > Energy Outputs	Creativity

Source: ©The Resilience Engine.

Here are my top energy maximisers that work for me:

o Really good quality time with my children, that is not filled with tasks.
o Really good quality time one-to-one with my husband.
o Sleep!
o Music, especially classical music, is a major topping-up factor. There are lots of options:
  • I can listen to 10 minutes of music and get a little top-up that helps just in that day.
  • If I listen to music every day, I get that top-up every day.
  • If I play music (I am a very amateur piano player, guitar player and singer), I get a real feeling of calm and connection with something very simple and nourishing in myself.
  • If I play music with others, boy, the payback is tenfold. Really good, I get energised by the connection made with no words. This is inspiring for me.
o Water. Being near it, walking next to it, especially the sea, but rivers and lakes are good too.
o Natural spaces, the bigger the better. Includes my garden, being on the hills, being in the mountains. Our holidays in the north of Scotland, an area of outstanding beauty and space, replenish me in a very deep way, across many months.

How to: Learn well

How you learn can be understood via David Kolb's model of learning.[30–32] Essentially, when learning, you:

1. **do** something
2. notice **what happened**

236

3. conclude by considering the **so what** of the situation
4. adapt and change in a new **what now?** plan to give it another go, but better this time around.

The learning process repeats in a spiral, in which your learning leads to better and better results:

LEARNING IN REALITY

Based on the Kolb Model

The key is to figure out which question you are comfortable answering – and which you seem to not have time for, or even actively avoid:

o   What shall I/we do?

The Resilience Engine finds that organisations are in a do-do-do mode very often. They therefore don't think enough and therefore don't learn.

o   What happened?

Specifically looking at the data of the event or situation. This is about being truthful with the facts, and seeing things for what they are. Without interpretation, and with intention of genuinely seeking all the data possible.

o So what? What might I/we conclude? Do we know we have the evidence for that? Where? What options do we have now, and what are the criteria for knowing which is best?

Concluding matters. With a real understanding of what happened, why, and what you can learn from this going forward.

o What now? As a result of understanding in step 3, what can we do now?

Planning. Not just jumping to the do-do-do, but ensuring that capacity is aligned, that all ducks are in a row as much as possible. Even if the planning is hold the intention of the outcome strongly – that can often be enough to start an experiment, then adjust as you go along.

Review

Here are some learning questions you might apply to your own and your team's thinking:

o What's it like for me/us to set time aside to review and reflect well?

o How can I/we stop falling into groupthink?

o What happens to my/our personal and group learning when negatively stressed?

o Do I review my/our learning at the end of the programme/ project?

o   How can I/we adopt an ongoing learning strategy?

o   How do I/we learn into the future? How much do I/we engage with imagination in this?

o   How can learning help me/us in my/our purpose?

How to: Purpose

©The Resilience Engine 2019

(✏) **Write down**

The Japanese concept of Ikigai[106] means 'what you live for' or the 'reason you leap out of bed in the morning'. Take some space to focus on yours.

Write down all the things that come into your head:

o   What do you love to do?

- What are you good at?
- What is important to you?
- What do you value about yourself and others?
- What is it about who you are and what you do that is important to others?

Now, set some time aside to reflect on your current goals. These could be work or home related or both. Jot them down. How do they connect to what matters to you? If you find it hard to make clear connections to your goals, particularly those that are, say, work and are therefore must-do's, think about how these contribute to your role.

 Commit

Commit to living more purposefully.

If your resilience is at Bounceback, connecting or indeed creating a clear, motivating, and real purpose for yourself is transformational. In the doing of this, you will start to say 'no' to things that you don't find energising and start to do a lot more of the things that you really do. This delivers high performance and wellbeing.

The Bottom Line

This chapter runs through very practically what to do at each different resilience level, plus examples of tools on the Top Enablers of resilience: being present, energy, learning and purpose. You can consider any of these ideas and tools for yourself and for your team.

End Words:
Resilience as a Practice

'Resilience is like a silver thread that runs through everything.'

'Resilience releases your creativity.'

Overview

By now you will know a lot about resilience and in particular your own resilience. You may also have used this book to explore with your team, to learn about the implications for your team's performance and wellbeing.

This short set of final words aims to help you get a really clear view of the core concepts of The Resilience Engine research and how to apply them day to day. In bringing all the key insights into one chapter, you can start to see how to create your own set of resilience habits, what we call a resilience practice. It is only with such a practice that you can achieve both high performance and wellbeing.

The Big 'Aha!'

The book has a key approach or method, called the 'Resilient Way'. It is based on the idea of using the lens of the core research model, the Resilience Dynamic®. This explains what resilience is.

Notably it applies to individuals, teams, organisations and any collective entity. We believe it can also apply to relationships, although this has not been fully researched!

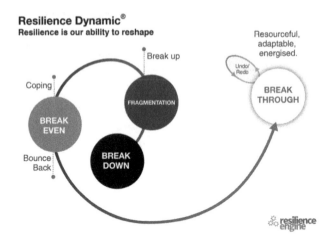

The use of the Resilience Dynamic® demystifies resilience. It illustrates its dynamic nature. It links all the different states of resilience, so you can see the connections between people who sometimes perform and sometimes cannot, or those high performers who do not fare well if forced to Cope due to context.

The model illustrates the straightforward definition of resilience as your ability to reshape, or your capacity for change, and thus the contiguous nature of resilience building from Coping upwards. The outcome of investing in resilience is so evidently a clear and practical pathway towards high performance and wellbeing, both without compromise.

The Resilience Dynamic® places resilience firmly in the field of leadership for high performance. It is strategically important for all leaders and managers, especially those leading significant change. Transformational change will not happen without resilience. Of crucial importance is the understanding that those who are not coping cannot embrace change, even if they would wish to; resilience boosting is required first. Understanding this is a game changer. The world of failed change management can be altered if this is taken into account: instead of forcing change through, first invest in resilience. As soon as people have levels of resilience from the middle of Breakeven upwards, change becomes possible. Higher resilience levels are where change is successful because it's coherent, supported and is done without the compromise of overwhelm or overwork.

Here are the details of why and how this happens.

The Top Twelve Insights on Resilience

1. Resilience is dynamic.

    There is nothing to shout about around this, it's entirely normal. High performers can experience a drop in resilience to Coping or lower levels. Those who have been stuck Coping for a long time can learn to improve their resilience levels and become healthier and more successful.

    See Chapters 5 and 8 for further details.

2. The measure of your resilience in any particular situation is dependent on both your **resilience potential** and the **resilience demands** of the multiple contexts in which you live and work. Change will only happen successfully if your resilience potential is equal to, or exceeds, the resilience demand.

    All sorts of factors affect the demand on your resilience: work pressures, family health issues etc. Different contexts trigger different reactions in you. Some are resilience enhancing, others are resilience draining.

A number of critical factors affect the availability of your resilience potential to meet these demands. The Top Enablers of being present, energy, learning and purpose are all at play.

See Chapters 5, 6, 8 and 9 for further details.

3. Resilience is not the domain for solely the clever or intellectual; learning how to support your resilience is available to everyone. Thus you can shift your resilience potential, ready for whatever resilience demand comes down the line.

   See Chapter 5 for further details.

4. High resilience involves shifting from reacting to proactively clarifying your intention. This means you proact to react intentionally.

   High-resilience people anticipate what might be coming down the line, and act before issues arise. They smooth out the bumps or issues before these arise.

   See Chapters 5, 6 and 7 for more.

5. Resilience investment can lead to a doubling of capacity.

   This only comes about by this smoothing of bumps. It means giving up on the rides of adrenalin-fuelled peaks and troughs, and swopping this for deep satisfaction, high performance and wellbeing.

   See Chapter 4 for more.

6. High resilience involves a significant investment in your Adaptive Capacity, the day-to-day fuel of your resilience.

    The golden rule is 65/35, where 35% of your time is invested into Adaptive Capacity: proactively gaining perspective in all sorts of ways; refreshing yourself most importantly through investment in your energy, and pacing yourself.

    See Chapters 4 and 9 for more.

7. Those with the highest resilience do not suffer the negative stress reaction, despite having the usual stressors. They are therefore not hijacked by the stress reaction, and remain resourceful no matter what is going on.

    See Chapter 7 for further details.

8. There are resilience myths that can hijack you. If you get caught or hooked by them, they will inhibit your resilience:
    *   From Myth 1: Resilience is not being tough.

        Toughness, which can lead long-term to brittleness, is the opposite of adaptability. The Resilient Way is all about creating options.

        See Chapter 1 for more detail.

    *   From Myth 2: Resilience is not becoming a control freak.

The relationship between resilience and control is not direct; you do not need one for the other. The Resilient Way is one of taking responsibility, and accountability as appropriate, and exercising control only if required and necessary.

See Chapter 2 for more detail.

- From Myth 3: Confidence is not an input to resilience.

   Confidence and resilience have a synergistic relationship where investment in one outputs the other. This depends on the specific aspect of confidence being discussed. Self-efficacy is an outcome of resilience; secure bases, those things that offer both security and inspiration, are both an input and outcome of the Resilient Way. The Resilience Engine calls this synergistic relationship a 'Generative Loop'.

   See Chapter 3 for more detail.

- From Myth 4: Driving efficiency delivers the highest productivity.

   Efficiency will only get you so far, and over-emphasis on an efficient set of processes will lead to diminishing returns. Resilience is needed for a lift in productivity.

   The Resilient Way includes tackling obvious inefficiencies. Thereafter, investment needs to be made in your Adaptive Capacity, the fuel of your resilience that gets used up day to day. By doing this you can double your capacity and release your creativity. These together deliver a transformative level of performance or productivity.

See Chapter 4 for more details.

9. Women's resilience seems to be lower than men's. Women are very strong copers, but not so good at investing in their own resilience. There is a tendency for 'superwoman' behaviour in women, which is resilience draining.

See Chapter 5 for further details.

10. There are three top barriers to resilience:
    * Not holding boundaries well which leads to a lack of safety.
    * Overestimating your capacity.
    * A do-it-yourself mindset which prevents you from asking for help.

See Chapter 7 and this chapter for further details.

11. There are three Top Enablers that are relevant across the Resilience Dynamic®, and a fourth that is particularly relevant from Bounceback upwards.
    * Being present. Being able to be here, right here, right now, no matter what else is going on. This skill needs to be cultivated.
    * Energy. A major contributor, energy follows the same ups and downs as resilience. This includes all areas of energy: physical, mental, emotional, spiritual.

- Learning. Not just what you learn but how you learn. You may often shortcut your learning, and this will constrain resilience.
- Purpose. This is about aligning work and life towards what is meaningful for you. And doing less of the stuff that drags you down.

See Chapters 9 and 10 for more details.

12. Resilience is not learnt as a one-off, it is a matter of practice.

The danger of diving into resilience in a big one-er is that the learning you take applies to the situations you find yourself in today. These won't be the same tomorrow.

The experience The Resilience Engine has with our clients is that their initial investments into resilience create fantastic results. However, clients then experience a disappointment when things slip back or get stuck. Ongoing investment in resilience via the Top Enablers is crucial for enabling a high, steady resilience level.

See the remainder of this chapter for further details of how to make resilience part of your day to day.

The Resilient Way: Resilience as a Practice

Resilience is a practice. It doesn't increase on the basis of a single event or intervention. Instead, a steady, ongoing and bite-sized way of connecting with the ideas and concepts of this book builds real resilience habits that stick. This is the Resilient Way.

Resilience gets developed through attention and experience. The contexts in which you draw on your resilience are varied:

Deliberately investing in taking time to rest

A set of senior leaders who it's tough to say 'no' to, but if you don't, you and your team's capacity for performance is severely under threat

Losing your keys every day!

Choosing to take time to exercise

Noticing and naming anger in the moment, but choosing not to be hijacked by it

Listening well to your kids

Thinking creatively about a particular problem

Allowing time to free-wheel, just notice, then assimilate your thoughts into useful stuff

Living with and indeed embracing the learning from the consequences of a health scare

Forgiving yourself and learning, so that you can move on

Saying 'no' to that cake or glass of wine, because it's better for your health.

This activity happens day in day out. Some big things, some small. Responding or proacting without drain in any of these situations, with ease is the Resilient Way.

Applying the Resilient Way

Know your why for resilience

© The Resilience Engine 2019

The first thing to do is to check out what is actually practical. All the best practice in the world shared by top performers in their field won't work for you if you can't sustain it. Sustaining it will only come if you really want the outcome of your investments, today and tomorrow.

🔍 Review

Consider what you want to invest most in day to day. Consider how the Top Enablers could help you practically in your own life:

Want to be present every day with someone?

o   With your kids?
o   With your partner?
o   With your team?

Want to maintain your energy?

o   Your physical energy, maybe improving your sleep? Consider having no or low-alcohol days, and be careful what you eat near bedtime; explore more of your own circadian rhythms!
o   Or just reconnecting with a bit of fun or joy in your life? Getting down the pub and having a laugh? Watching funny films with your kids?!
o   Or recovering your energy at a deep level, maybe seeking a real way of quietening the mind down?

Want to reconnect with learning more often?

o Just get curious again? Get out and about, see what you fancy, where your mind and body takes you?

o Fancy getting better at something? Like a sport, or eating more healthily?

o Want to be stimulated via others so you can get that buzz, that spring, that oomph, that wow of discovery?

o Doing something way out of your comfort zone and seeing what it's like right out on the edge of learning again?

Want to connect with your purpose on a more day-to-day basis?

o With your service users? With your clients? Meeting them on a regular basis? Listening to them over lunch?

o With your colleagues? About why what you do matters so much? Even if you're not yet doing it really well, connecting with others who seek to improve things around you?

o With your family, really properly? Because they're the ones for whom you bust your gut day in day out?

Planning your Resilience Practice

©The Resilience Engine 2019

✐ Write down
Without a Resilience Practice Plan your intentions can get hijacked.

Write down what you will do for your resilience and how often. Here's an example from Alison Kane, Director of Services at The Resilience Engine:

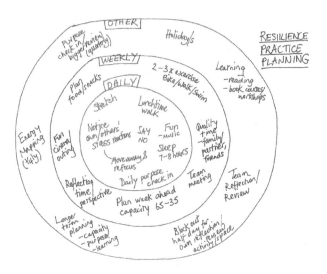

You can use the same three concentric circles. Draw them on the page, and decide what routines you are going to put in, for real, that will support your resilience day to day.

✔ **Commit**

What parts of your plan will you actually fully commit to? What help or resources do you need to be able to do this?

Last Words

This book is all about how to achieve both high performance and wellbeing, both without compromise. The ticket to that is your resilience, and the pathway feels like stepping through a 'resilience gateway'. One side of this gateway can feel pretty complicated; the other side is very straightforward.

Living your life in a Resilient Way is simple. It means investing in your resilience day to day which in turn means investing in

252

your wellbeing. That is practical, doable and learnable. Of course life will throw up new challenges for you to deal with. With the Resilient Way, you will be ready for these, and smooth many out before they rise to become difficult.

The Resilient Way means rejecting the cultural myths of resilience, such as being tough, or having to be in complete control in all situations. Instead resilience is about you investing in your flexibility, your adaptability.

The purpose of this book has been to demystify all of this and boil it down to something straightforward so that you can achieve high performance and wellbeing. You can feel at ease as a result, you and your team. I hope I have achieved this boiling down process. And I hope you have achieved the boiling down for yourself and your resilience. Living the Resilient Way is healthy, energetic, successful and joyous. I wish that absolutely for you.

You may have many other questions and the team at The Resilience Engine would be delighted to respond. We work with organisations, leaders and managers, to help them connect for real with their own resilience, so they can achieve both high performance and wellbeing. We would be delighted to work with you. Please see Resources for further information and contact details.

About the Author

Jenny Campbell is an executive coach and resilience researcher. Resilience is a fundamental learning capability that gives rise to both high performance and wellbeing, both without compromise. Jenny has dedicated her practice to furthering the understanding of resilience, knowing that you can achieve both, despite the pressures and volatility in our world. This is the Resilient Way.

Jenny formed the company, The Resilience Engine, to bring the company's ten years of research to organisations and make her vision of 'Resilience for Everyone' a reality. The company works with organisations to enable their full workforce in performance and wellbeing, helping staff, managers and leaders. The Resilience Engine helps organisations build and enable a resilient culture via consulting, coaching and services such as blended learning. These services have been proven to be very impactful: 100% of clients say the insights are relevant to them, and 85% of those using The Resilience Engine's eLearning guides and toolkits say they would recommend these to others.

The Resilience Engine sees itself as a nexus in a growing network of contributors to the performance and wellbeing of our people and economy. Our partners include The Academy of Executive Coaching, experts in training coaches and internal HR/Organisational Development practitioners in coaching skills, plus The Healthy Workforce, an organisation enabling the wellbeing of the workforce through a model of wellbeing called STEM, Sleep-Think-Eat-Move. The Resilience Engine works to collaborate and innovate, and hopes that the waves it creates through the Resilient Way of working and living will help replenish and support adaptation of our world during our turbulent times.

Jenny lives and breathes all of this. Her family believes in it all too.

See www.resilienceengine.com for more information on the company.

For services, please see http://www.resilienceengine.com/our-services/.

My Thanks

Thank you to all the clients of The Resilience Engine. We are grateful for the trust you have placed in a small team with a big ambition.

Thank you to The Resilience Engine clients, colleagues and partners such as The Academy of Executive Coaching[3] and Anne Archer of The Healthy Workforce[108] who have taken part in our action enquiry research conversations across the years. You are all generous and insightful!

Thanks to the growing Resilience Engine Community of Practice whose members, professional coaches and internal coaches/Organisational Development consultants, have each agreed to get fully dunked in how to apply The Resilience Engine research findings in their own practice. You are critical to our efforts in stretching our understanding of resilience and how to apply it.

Thanks to The Resilience Engine core team: Alison Kane, Calum Murray, Serena Battistoni and Sofi Armitage, who are creators, challengers and resilient! You have helped drive the quality of our services, and have provided significant input into the book.

Thanks to my family and friends who have been behind me every step of the way in my resilience journey. I love you all for putting up with me.

Finally, to my husband Patrick and my children Mara and Euan, thank you for believing in me.

The Resilience Engine
Research Method

The Resilience Engine has been researching resilience since 2007. In that time our understanding of research methods has grown and developed. As real-world practitioners in the field of executive coaching and leadership development, we have at each stage of research taken a pragmatic approach whilst maintaining rigour in our methodology. At all times we have been supervised in our work. The prime research method we adopt is one that enables a co-enquiry with our research clients. This qualitative research method is 'Action Enquiry',[109,110] where both researcher and client lean in together to discover what resilience means and how to build it, within that client's context. Within this the researcher must account for the reflexivity in the data collection and analysis.

The initial literature review within The Resilience Engine research established what existing academic knowledge and resilience theories already existed, in order to shape a coherent hypothesis.

With this hypothesis a set of interviews with leaders was carried out, with the enquiry of whether this hypothesis would bear out in practice. It didn't take long to establish that it did not!

The theory based on hypothesis didn't last through even the first interview before being proven as flawed. As lead researcher, I threw away the idea of using a theoretical hypothesis and instead embarked on learning about Grounded Research methodology. This is a qualitative research method, based on people's lived experiences. It has formed the basis of The Resilience Engine research method since that time.

The Resilience Engine research data now is built from hundreds of stories, plus hundreds of pieces of data from academic and written literature. Each data piece goes into a big melting pot and is analysed using Grounded Theory[111–114] methods (where any story or piece of data is reviewed from the ground up and coded according to common themes and patterns that arise) and more recently using Charmaz's extension of this, Constructivist Grounded Theory[115,116] methods (where stories are correlated against a particular theory using abductive reasoning techniques, where the theory informs the data sought, but data then informs the theory development). Each of these methods seeks to understand patterns and connections between all the data. The process of coding the data into themes is repeated again and again, seeking further data if necessary, until there is what is known as 'saturation', whereby whatever angle you come at something or other from, the data shows the same pattern or insight. That's the moment we as researchers can determine that there is validation or a believable insight from the research.

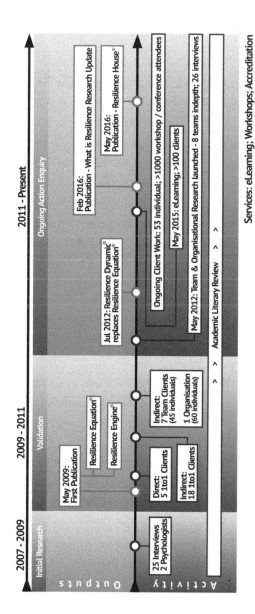

©The Resilience Engine

The Resilience Engine original data sample included:

o Initial 25 interviews with leaders, with the supervision of two psychologists. This gave rise to The Resilience Engine® as a model, and also to an earlier version of the Resilience Dynamic® called the Resilience Equation. The research methodology was based on Grounded Theory.

o A validation process with 1–1 and team clients, with stories from 128 individual clients. This validated The Resilience Engine® model itself, but demonstrated that the Resilience Equation was woefully inadequate; it was replaced in 2012 by the Resilience Dynamic®. The research methodology used was influenced by Constructivist Grounded Theory.

o A further research programme into team and organisational resilience using Grounded Theory methods. This was kicked off in 2012, and has had two phases already, because of its complexity.

- Phase 1: 2012–2015
  - Working in-depth with 8 teams totalling 74 team members across several months in a co-enquiry on team resilience. Grounded Theory research methods were used.
  - 26 individual and team interviews covering 68 different organisations undertaken using Constructivist Grounded Theory techniques.
  - Many insights have been borne from this data which we incorporate into our consulting and coaching practice. There are a number of research sub-questions that remain outstanding in this work.
- Phase 2: 2016
  - A more in-depth review of academic literature on team and organisational resilience encompassing

aspects of high performance and change. This was in search of more data regarding:

- Performance in different organisational structures (hierarchical, collaborative, networked etc)
- Performance versus different ownership models (PLC, Public, Family Business, Partnership etc).

- Phase 3: 2017
    - Started to re-initiate and shape a further final phase into the Action Enquiry with teams, but had to stop with the sudden death of our research supervisor in 2017; it is expected to restart end 2019/early 2020.

Since the original publications of 2009 and validation process, the research enquiry has continued. As Glaser,[113–117] the original developer of Grounded Theory methods, said, 'all is data'. All written articles, books, interviews, stories, observations and self-reflexive insights are considered data for Grounded Theory. We therefore continue to sit with data drawn from client work, reading and stories at least once per year. The data we review includes:

o All client and practitioner stories from our growing Resilience Engine Community of Practice.[35] Each practitioner must offer multiple case studies as part of their submission for accreditation. With over 60 practitioners, we have hundreds of stories from this source.

o The Resilience Engine clients themselves. We have worked with hundreds of clients across the years, and continue yearly to document insights and findings. These have spun off particular questions that are currently under investigation which include:

- How do the links to wellbeing and resilience work at each resilience level?

- What are the implications for women of different ages, particularly menopausal women?
- All new insights or questions from our ongoing reading into the field.

If you have any questions regarding our research methodology, please contact info@resilienceengine.com.

Resources

1. The Resilience Check-in©

You are welcome to complete a simple yet comprehensive self-evaluation of your resilience levels using The Resilience Engine's 'Resilience Check-in' tool. There is a link on our homepage: www.resilienceengine.com. Feel free to give it a go.

2. Monthly resilience publications

If you have found the insights from this book helpful and want help with how to apply the Resilient Way on an ongoing basis, The Resilience Engine has a monthly set of publications that you can receive for free. Please go to our website and search under Resources: http://www.resilienceengine.com/resources/publications/. You will be prompted for your email details, and can sign up to receive our Being Resilient publication.

We have additional specialised publications that may be more pertinent to your needs. To receive either our Resilience Coaching or Enabling the Resilient Organisation publications, please email us directly to find out which publications would be most appropriate to your needs. Email: info@resilienceengine.com.

3. Resilience Engine services

The Resilience Engine works to make the research insights available for everyone. We have face-to-face and blended services for different sets of the workforce:

o   Resilience Coaching for leaders and managers

o   Resilience Being Resilient Workshop Series, tailored as appropriate

o   Blended services: **Resilience Made Simple** for all staff, and **Build Resilience Habits** for managers.

See www.resilienceengine.com for more information on the company.

For services, please see specifically: http://www.resilienceengine.com/our-services/.

4. Join The Resilience Engine Community of Practice

If you are interested in becoming one of The Resilience Engine Community of Practice, or indeed want to build a resilience support capability in-house, please see details of our Accreditation programme. This is delivered either in-house or as a public programme in partnership with the Academy of Executive Coaching:

http://www.resilienceengine.com/community-of-practice/

5. To understand more about The Resilience Engine research methods

Please see the Research tab on the main menu of our website: http://www.resilienceengine.com/research-method/

References

1. Goleman, D. Train Your Brain for Flow. *Linkedin Pulse* (2016).

2. Csikszentmihalyi, M. The Flow of Thought. In *Flow: The Psychology of Optimal Experience.* (Harper Perennial Modern Classics, 2008).

3. AOEC. The Academy of Executive Coaching. Available at: https://www.aoec.com/.

4. McDermott, J. O. and I. *The Principles of NLP.* 84 (Singing Dragon, 2013).

5. Kohlrieser, G. *Hostage at the Table.* (Jossey-Bass, 2006).

6. Campbell, J. (The Research Engine). What is Resilience? 1–8 (2015).

7. Covey, S. *The 7 Habits of Highly Effective People.* (Simon & Schuster, 2004).

8. Bandura, A. Self-efficacy mechanism in human agency. *Am. Psychol.* (1982). doi:10.1037/0003-066X.37.2.122

9. Bandura, A. Human agency in social cognitive theory. *Am. Psychol.* (1989). doi:10.1037/0003-066X.44.9.1175

10. Bandura, A. Social cognitive theory. In *Handbook of Theories of Social Psychology: Volume 1.* (2012). doi:10.4135/97814462 49215.n18

11. Bandura, A. Self-efficacy: Toward a unifying theory of behavioral change. *Adv. Behav. Res. Ther.* (1978). doi:10.1016/0146-6402(78)90002-4

12. McLeod, S. Bandura – Social learning theory. *SimplyPsychology. org* (2016).

13. Kohlrieser, G. & Goldsworthy, S. *Care to Dare: Unleashing Astonishing Potential through Secure-Base Leadership.* (John Wiley & Sons, 2012).

14. Howe, D. Handbook of attachment: Theory, research and clinical applications. *Journal of Social Work* (2009). doi:10.1177/1468017309342543

15. Shahar-Maharik, T. & Oppenheim, D. Attachment. In *Encyclopedia of Mental Health: Second Edition.* (2015). doi:10.1016/B978-0-12-397045-9.00228-7

16. Holmes, J. *John Bowlby and Attachment Theory.* (2014). doi:10.4324/9781315879772

17. Hughes, R., Kinder, A. & Cooper, C. L. *The Wellbeing Workout.* (2018). doi:10.1007/978-3-319-92552-3

18. Wagnild, G. M. & Young, H. M. Development and psychometric evaluation of the Resilience Scale. *J. Nurs. Meas.* (1993).

19. Hultell, D. & Gustavsson, J. P. A psychometric evaluation of the Scale of Work Engagement and Burnout (SWEBO). *Work* (2010). doi:10.3233/WOR-2010-1078

20. Clough, P., Earle, K. & Strycharczyk, D. Developing resilience through coaching: MTQ48. In *Psychometrics in Coaching: Using Psychological and Psychometric Tools for Development.* (Kogan Page, 2008).

21. Perry, J. L., Clough, P. J., Crust, L., Earle, K. & Nicholls, A. R. Factorial validity of the Mental Toughness Questionnaire-48. *Pers. Individ. Dif.* (2013). doi:10.1016/j.paid.2012.11.020

22. Dweck, C. *Mindset. The New Psychology of Success.* (Random House Publishing Group, 2008).

23. Campbell, J. (The Research Engine). Personal and Organisational Resilience. 1–16 (2009).

24. Fletcher, D. & Sarkar, M. A grounded theory of psychological resilience in Olympic champions. *Psychol. Sport Exerc.* (2012). doi:10.1016/j.psychsport.2012.04.007

25. Kanter, R. M. Column: Cultivate a culture of confidence. *Harv. Bus. Rev.* (2011).

26. Kanter, R. M. *Confidence*. (Crown Business, 2006).

27. Du Plessis, R., Sutherland, J., Gordon, L. & Gibson, H. 'The confidence to know I can survive': Resilience and recovery in post-quake Christchurch. *Kotuitui* (2015). doi:10.1080/11770 83X.2015.1071712

28. Wikipedia.

29. Thurmon, D. *Off Balance on Purpose: Embrace Uncertainty and Create a Life you Love*. (Greenleaf, 2010).

30. Vince, R. Behind and beyond Kolb's learning cycle. *J. Manag. Educ.* (1998). doi:10.1177/105256299802200304

31. Kolb, D., Stumpf, S. & Freedman, R. Experiential learning theory and the Learning Style Inventory: A reply to Freedman and Stumpf/'The Learning Style Inventory: Still less than meets the eye. *Acad. Manag. Rev.* (1981).

32. Mcleod, S. Kolb's learning styles and experiential learning cycle | Simply Psychology. *Creative Commons* (2017). doi:10.1136/ lupus-2015-000113

33. Wong, T. Digital Onion. Available at: https://digitalonion.com/ company/.

34. Carlisle, A. E. MacGregor. *Organizational Dynamics* (1995).

35. Resilience Engine Community of Practice. Available at: http:// www.resilienceengine.com/community-of-practice/.

36. MAPPG. *Mindful Nation UK. The Mindfulness Initiative* (2015).

37. Wikipedia. Command and control. Available at: https:// en.wikipedia.org/wiki/Command_and_control.

38. Ayers, S. Birth trauma and post-traumatic stress disorder: The importance of risk and resilience. *J. Reprod. Infant Psychol.* (2017). doi:10.1080/02646838.2017.1386874

39. Ong, A. D., Standiford, T. & Deshpande, S. Hope and stress resilience. In *The Oxford Handbook of Hope*. (Oxford University Press, 2018).

40. Priel, A., Djalovski, A., Zagoory-Sharon, O. & Feldman, R. Maternal depression impacts child psychopathology across the first decade of life: Oxytocin and synchrony as markers of resilience. *J. Child Psychol. Psychiatry Allied Discip.* (2019). doi:10.1111/jcpp.12880

41. Mistretta, E. G. *et al.* Resilience training for work-related stress among health care workers. *J. Occup. Environ. Med.* (2018). doi:10.1097/JOM.0000000000001285

42. Berg, C. J. *et al.* Resilience and biomarkers of health risk in Black smokers and nonsmokers. *Heal. Psychol.* (2017). doi:10.1037/hea0000540

43. Svendsen, E. Cultivating resilience: Urban stewardship as a means to improving health and well-being. *Restor. Commons Creat. Heal. Well-Being Through Urban Landscapes* (2009).

44. McGinnis, D. Resilience, life events, and well-being during midlife: Examining resilience subgroups. *J. Adult Dev.* (2018). doi:10.1007/s10804-018-9288-y

45. Theiss, J. A. Family communication and resilience. *J. Appl. Commun. Res.* (2018). doi:10.1080/00909882.2018.1426706

46. Velthorst, E., Reichenberg, A., Rabinowitz, J. & Levine, S. Z. Study of resilience and environmental adversity in midlife health (STREAM). *Soc. Psychiatry Psychiatr. Epidemiol.* (2015). doi:10.1007/s00127-015-1126-y

47. Greitens, E. *Resilience. Hard-won Wisdom for Living a Better Life.* (Houghton Mifflin, 2015).

48. Jennison, J. *Leading through Uncertainty: Emotional Resilience and Human Connection in a Performance-driven World.* (Practical Inspiration Publishing, 2018).

49. Barry, D. H. *Emotional Resilience: How to Safeguard Your Mental Health.* (Orion Spring, 2018).

50. Sandberg, S. G. A. *Option B: Facing Adversity, Building Resilience and Finding Joy.* (WH Allen, 2017).

51. Duckworth, A. *Grit: Why Passion and Resilience Are the Secrets to Success.* (Vermilion, 2017).

52. Paustian-Underdahl, S. C., Walker, L. S. & Woehr, D. J. Gender and perceptions of leadership effectiveness: A meta-analysis of contextual moderators. *J. Appl. Psychol.* (2014). doi:10.1037/a0036751

53. Sandberg, S. *Lean In: Women, Work, and the Will to Lead.* (WH Allen, 2013).

54. Mohr, T. S. Why women don't apply for jobs unless they're 100% qualified. *Harvard Business Review* (2014).

55. Clance, P. R. & Imes, S. A. The imposter phenomenon in high achieving women: Dynamics and therapeutic intervention. *Psychother. Theory, Res. Pract.* (2007). doi:10.1037/h0086006

56. Digital Science *et al. Championing the Success of Women in Science, Technology, Engineering, Maths, and Medicine* (2017).

57. Wax, R. *Sane New World: Taming the Mind.* (Hodder and Stoughton, 2013).

58. Tsipursky, D. G. *The Truth-Seeker's Handbook: A Science-Based Guide.* (Bowker, 2017).

59. Karlsson, N., Loewenstein, G. & Seppi, D. The ostrich effect: Selective attention to information. *J. Risk Uncertain.* (2009). doi:10.1007/s11166-009-9060-6

60. Wikipedia. The ostrich effect. Available at: https://en.wikipedia.org/wiki/Ostrich_effect.

61. Nickerson, R. S. Confirmation bias: A ubiquitous phenomenon in many guises. *Rev. Gen. Psychol.* (1998). doi:10.1037/1089-2680.2.2.175

62. Johnson, D. K. Confirmation bias. In *Bad Arguments: 50 Common Fallacies and How to Avoid Them.* (2017). doi:10.1002/9781119165811.ch73

63. Klayman, J. Varieties of confirmation bias. *Psychol. Learn. Motiv. - Adv. Res. Theory* (1995). doi:10.1016/S0079-7421(08)60315-1

64. Rajsic, J., Wilson, D. E. & Pratt, J. Confirmation bias in visual search. *J. Exp. Psychol. Hum. Percept. Perform.* (2015). doi:10.1037/xhp0000090

65. Strough, J. N., Mehta, C. M., McFall, J. P. & Schuller, K. L. Are older adults less subject to the sunk-cost fallacy than younger adults? Short report. *Psychol. Sci.* (2008). doi:10.1111/j.1467-9280.2008.02138.x

66. Haita-Falah, C. Sunk-cost fallacy and cognitive ability in individual decision-making. *J. Econ. Psychol.* (2017). doi:10.1016/j.joep.2016.12.001

67. Olivola, C. Y. The interpersonal sunk-cost effect. *Psychol. Sci.* (2018). doi:10.1177/0956797617752641

68. Gino, F. Do we listen to advice just because we paid for it? The impact of advice cost on its use. *Organ. Behav. Hum. Decis. Process.* (2008). doi:10.1016/j.obhdp.2008.03.001

69. Wheaton, B. & Montazer, S. Stressors, stress, and distress. In *A Handbook for the Study of Mental Health.* (2012). doi:10.1017/cbo9780511984945.013

70. Oken, B. S., Chamine, I. & Wakeland, W. A systems approach to stress, stressors and resilience in humans. *Behavioural Brain Research* (2015). doi:10.1016/j.bbr.2014.12.047

71. Center, J. H. S. Understanding what happens when you sleep. Available at: https://www.hopkinsmedicine.org/health/healthy-sleep/sleep-science/the-science-of-sleep-understanding-what-happens-when-you-sleep.

72. John Hopkins Medicine. Your top sleep questions answered.

73. McGonigal, K. The science of willpower (TED). *Harv. Bus. Rev.* (2014).

74. McGonigal, K. How to make stress your friend. *TEDGlobal* (2013).

75. McGonigal, K. How to make stress your friend | TED Talk. *TEDGlobal* (2013).

76. McGonigal, K. *The Upside of Stress: Why Stress is Good for You (and How to Get Good at It)*. (Vermilion, 2015).

77. Brown, B. *Daring Greatly: How the Courage to Be Vulnerable Transforms the Way We Live, Love, Parent, and Lead.* (Penguin Random House, 2015).

78. Sharma, R. R. & Cooper, S. C. Stress and burnout: An introduction. In *Executive Burnout.* (2017). doi:10.1108/978-1-78635-286-620161001

79. Sharma, R. R. & Cooper, S. C. Models of burnout. In *Executive Burnout.* (2017). doi:10.1108/978-1-78635-286-620161004

80. McKinsey & Company. Organizing for successful change management: A McKinsey Global Survey. *McKinsey Q.* (2006).

81. Boaz, N. & Fox, E. A. Change leader, change thyself. *McKinsey Q.* (2014).

82. Keller, S. & Aiken, C. The inconvenient truth about change management. *Mckinsey & Company* (2008).

83. McKinsey & Company. Creating organizational transformations. *McKinsey Q.* (2008).

84. McKinsey & Company & Peters, T. Tom Peters on leading the 21st-century organization. *McKinsey Q.* (2014).

85. Kirschner, H. *et al.* Soothing your heart and feeling connected: A new experimental paradigm to study the benefits of self-compassion. *Clin. Psychol. Sci.* (2019). doi:10.1177/2167702618812438

86. Whitehead, P. M. The runner's high revisited: A phenomenological analysis. *J. Phenomenol. Psychol.* (2016). doi:10.1163/15691624-12341313

87. Amir, O. Tough choices: How making decisions tires your brain. *Sci. Am.* (2008).

88. Levitin, D. *The Organized Mind: Thinking Straight in the Age of Information Overload.* (Penguin, 2015).

89. Barsh, J., Mogelof, J. & Webb, C. How centered leaders achieve extraordinary results. *McKinsey Q.* (2010). doi:10.1071/WR9830373

90. Amabile, T. M. & Kramer, S. J. How leaders kill meaning at work. *McKinsey Q.* (2012).

91. Basford, T. & Schaninger, B. Winning hearts and minds in the 21st century. *McKinsey Q.* (2016).

92. Oswald, A. J., Proto, E. & Sgroi, D. Happiness and productivity. *J. Labor Econ.* (2015). doi:10.1086/681096

93. Caillet, A. & Hirshberg, J. How your state of mind affects your performance. *Harv. Bus. Rev.* (2014).

94. Huselid, M. A. The impact of human resource management practices on turnover, productivity, and corporate financial performance. *Acad. Manag. J.* (2018). doi:10.5465/256741

95. Thrash, T. M. & Elliot, A. J. Inspiration as a psychological construct. *J. Pers. Soc. Psychol.* (2003). doi:10.1037/0022-3514.84.4.871

96. Thrash, T. M. & Elliot, A. J. Inspiration: Core characteristics, component processes, antecedents, and function. *J. Pers. Soc. Psychol.* (2004). doi:10.1037/0022-3514.87.6.957

97. Elliot, A. J. & Thrash, T. M. Achievement goals and the hierarchical model of achievement motivation. *Educ. Psychol. Rev.* (2001). doi:10.1023/A:1009057102306

98. Elliot, A. J., Thrash, T. M. & Murayama, K. A Longitudinal analysis of self-regulation and well-being: Avoidance personal goals, avoidance coping, stress generation, and subjective well-being. *J. Pers. Soc. Psychol.* (2011). doi:10.1111/j.1467-6494.2011.00694.x

99. Valikangas, L. *The Resilient Organization: How Adaptive Cultures Thrive Even When Strategy Fails.* (McGraw-Hill Professional, 2010).

100. Scharmer, O. *Theory U: Leading from the Future as It Emerges.* (Berrett-Koehler Publishers, 2016).

101. Sinek, S. *Start with Why: How Great Leaders Inspire Everyone to Take Action.* (Penguin, 2011).

102. Sinek, S. *Start with Why.* (Penguin, 2011).

103. Stanford. Steve Jobs' 2005 Stanford Commencement Address. *YouTube* (2005). Available at: https://youtu.be/UF8uR6Z6KLc.

104. Taylor, S. *The Leap: The Psychology of Spiritual Awakening.* (New World Library, 2017).

105. Casserley, T. *Learning from Burnout.* (Routledge, 2008).

106. García, H. & Miralles, F. *Ikigai: The Japanese Secret to a Long and Happy Life.* (Hutchinson, 2017).

107. Burton, D. & Raedeke, T. D. Sport psychology for coaches. *Int. J. Sport. Sci. Coach.* (2008). doi:10.1260/174795408785100734

108. Archer, A. The Healthy Workforce. Available at: https://www.linkedin.com/in/annearcher/?originalSubdomain=uk.

109. Silverman, D. *Qualitative Research.* (Sage, 2016).

110. Silverman, D. *Doing Qualitative Research.* (Sage, 2013).

111. Khan, S. N. Qualitative research method: Grounded theory. *Int. J. Bus. Manag.* (2014). doi:10.5539/ijbm.v9n11p224

112. Charmaz, K. Grounded theory as an emergent method. In *Handbook of Emergent Methods.* (2008). doi:10.1002/9781405 165518.wbeosg070.pub2

113. Haig, B. D. Grounded theory method. In *Studies in Applied Philosophy, Epistemology and Rational Ethics.* (2018). doi:10.1007/978-3-030-01051-5_5

114. Taylor, B. Grounded theory. In *Qualitative Research in the Health Sciences: Methodologies, Methods and Processes.* (2013). doi:10.4324/9780203777176

115. Charmaz, K. *Constructing Grounded Theory: A Practical Guide Through Qualitative Analysis.* (Sage, 2006).

116. Charmaz, K. & Bryant, A. Grounded theory. In *International Encyclopedia of Education*. (2010). doi:10.1016/B978-0-08-044894-7.01581-5

117. Glaser, B. Basics of grounded theory analysis. *Recherche* (1992).